MICHELLE OBAMA BIOGRAPHY

A Beacon of Strength and Inspiration

Note:

....

....

....

....

....

Jeremy Ray Hulburt

CONTENTS

INTRODUCTION

There may be no tidy solutions or pithy answers to life's big challenges, but Michelle Obama believes that we can all locate and lean on a set of tools to help us better navigate change and remain steady within flux. In The Light We Carry, she opens a frank and honest dialogue with readers, considering the questions many of us wrestle with: How do we build enduring and honest relationships? How can we discover strength and community inside our differences? What tools do we use to address feelings of self-doubt or helplessness? What do we do when it all starts to feel like too much?

Michelle Obama offers readers a series of fresh stories and insightful reflections on change, challenge, and power, including her belief that when we light up for others, we can illuminate the richness and potential of the world around us, discovering deeper truths and new pathways for progress. Drawing from her experiences as a mother, daughter, spouse, friend, and First Lady, she shares the habits and principles she has developed to successfully adapt to change and overcome various obstacles—the earned wisdom that helps her continue to "become." She details her most valuable practices, like "starting kind," "going high," and assembling a "kitchen table" of trusted friends and mentors. With trademark humour, candour, and compassion, she also explores issues connected to race, gender, and visibility, encouraging readers to work through fear, find strength in community, and live with boldness."When we are able to recognize our own light, we become empowered to use it," writes Michelle Obama. A rewarding blend of powerful stories and profound advice that will ignite conversation, The Light We Carry inspires readers to examine their own lives, identify their sources of gladness, and connect meaningfully in a turbulent world.

CHAPTER 1

START AGAIN

As time passed, our family settled into a calm pattern, anchored by longer-than-usual evening dinners. We'd discuss the news, comparing notes on what we'd heard or read—the day's depressing numbers or the unsettlingly unpredictable rhetoric emanating from the White House, our previous home. We played the board games I'd purchased, did some puzzles, and watched movies on the couch. We laughed whenever we found something to joke about. Because otherwise, it was all too frightening. This moment of silence and seclusion was quite difficult for me, as I'm sure it was for many others. It felt like a trap door opened into a stew of fears that I couldn't make sense of or manage. At that point, I'd spent a lifetime staying busy—keeping busy—in part, I believe, to feel some feeling of control. I'd always lived by lists, agendas, and strategic plans, both at business and at home. I utilised them as a road map, a way to know where I was heading in order to get there as quickly as possible. I might be a little obsessed with making and quantifying progress.

However, the initial months of the pandemic bulldozed all of this. It pulled the framework of my days away. My usual lists, calendars, and strategic plans were suddenly clogged with cancellations, postponements, and big maybes. When friends called, it was usually to discuss what was bothering them. Every future plan now included an asterisk. An asterisk appeared to be tied to the future. Some of those old feelings had resurfaced. Just when I thought I'd worked things out, I found myself lost and out of control once more. It felt as if I had arrived in a city devoid of street signs and landmarks. Should I turn right or left? Which direction is downtown? I'd gotten disoriented. I'd also lost some of my armour as a result.

When I eventually got around to picking up the two beginner-size knitting needles I'd ordered online, I was in a bad mood. When I unrolled a short piece of the thick grey yarn I'd bought and looped it over a needle for the first time, tying it with a tiny slipknot before beginning a second loop, I was struggling with a sensation of hopelessness—of not-enoughness.

I had always assumed that my head was entirely in charge of everything, even ordering my hands what to do, in all my decades of staying busy. It had never occurred to me to let things flow in the opposite direction. But that's exactly what knitting did. It caused the flow to be reversed. It sat my racing mind in the back seat and let my hands operate the car for a while. It diverted my attention away from my anxiousness long enough to bring some relief. I could feel the rearrangement every time I picked up those needles, my fingers doing the work and my mind lagging behind. I continued to perform the job I'd been doing—speaking at virtual voter registration drives, supporting good causes, addressing people's pain—but personally, I was finding it more difficult to access my own hope or feel like I could actually make a difference. Democratic leadership had approached me about giving a speech at the party's national convention in mid-August, but I hadn't yet agreed. I felt stopped whenever I thought about it, caught up in my indignation and grief for what we'd already lost as a country. I couldn't imagine saying anything. I was enveloped with gloom.

What's possibly unusual is that I'm not sure I'd have gotten there without the period of forced quiet and the steadiness I discovered inside knitting. I'd had to start small before I could dream big again. Shaken by the enormity of what was going on, I needed my hands to reacquaint me to what was good, basic, and doable. And it turned out to be quite a lot. You can't always see where you're going when you start something new. You must be cool with not knowing how things will turn out. Cast on your first stitch and follow a chart—a series of letters and numbers that may appear obscure and unintelligible to a non-knitter. The chart instructs you on which stitches to place in what order, but it takes some time before you can see anything adding up—before the design actually becomes evident in the yarn. Until then, you simply move your hands and follow the directions. It's an act of trust in this sense. Which reminds me that it's not that trivial after all. We put our faith into action in the tiniest of ways. And by doing so, we remind ourselves of what is possible. We're saying, "I can" with it. We are saying, "I care." We are not giving up. In knitting, as in so much else in life, I've discovered that the only way to get to your greater answer is to put down one tiny stitch at a time. You sew and stitch and stitch again until you've completed a row. You stitch your second row above your first, your third row above your second, and your fourth row above your third. With time and effort, you will be able to see the form itself. You see an answer—that thing you longed for—a fresh arrangement taking shape in your hands.

And for a brief moment, you can understand that it matters—that what you've created is perfectly enough.

Maybe that counts as progress.

At least, I hope so.

So, let's get started.

CHAPTER 2

OVERCOME FEAR

I was fortunate to grow up in a pretty safe and stable environment, surrounded by people I could trust, and I'm conscious that it provided me with a certain baseline for understanding what safety and stability feel like—an advantage that not everyone has. When it comes to being terrified, there's a lot I don't see and a lot I don't know about other people's experiences. The majority of what I'm saying here is abstract fear—fear of embarrassment or rejection, concerns that something will go wrong or that someone will be hurt. What I've realised is that danger is woven into the human experience, regardless of who you are, what you look like, or where you live.

When you think about it, fear frequently arises in this manner as an instinctive response to disorder and difference, to the introduction of anything new or frightening into our awareness. It can be completely sensible in some cases and quite irrational in others. That is why how we learn to filter it is so important. As we become older, our reactions to fear, stress, and other threatening situations become more sophisticated. We may not scream and run away like we did as children, but we still retreat in different ways. The adult equivalent of a child's shriek is avoidance. Perhaps you do not apply for a promotion at work. You don't walk across the room to meet someone you admire. You don't enrol in a class that will challenge you or engage in a conversation with someone whose political or religious ideas you are unfamiliar with. In order to avoid the anxiety and discomfort of taking a risk, you may be passing up a chance. You are shrinking your universe by clinging to what you know. You are denying yourself opportunities to progress.

I believe it is always worthwhile to question yourself, "Am I afraid because I am in actual danger, or am I afraid because I am confronted with newness?" Decoding fear entails pausing to analyse our own instincts, assessing what we move away from and what we might more easily step toward, and, perhaps most importantly, why we step forward or back. These can also be applied to bigger socio economic issues. We are more prone to seek for and value features of sameness in our life when we shun what is new or different and allow those urges in ourselves to go unquestioned. We may build groups based on similarity; we may accept uniformity as a form of comfort, a means of avoiding danger. And so, when we immerse ourselves in the sameness, we are only surprised by the difference. We become less acclimated to anything—or anyone—who is unfamiliar to us.

I think the most nervous I've ever felt in my life was the first time Barack informed me he intended to run for President of the United States. I was terrified by the possibility of it. Worse, as we talked off and on over the course of a few weeks late in 2006, he made it obvious that the decision was entirely up to me. He loved me, he needed me, and we worked well together. That is, if I thought the venture was too hazardous or would cause too many problems for our family, I could call it quits.

All I had to do was refuse. And, believe me, even though everyone around us was pressing Barack to run, I was ready to call it quits. But I felt that before I did, I owed him—and us—an honest reckoning with the decision. I had to reason my way through the immediate shock. I needed to sort through my fears and locate my most sensible thoughts. For a number of weeks, I carried this seemingly absurd and terrifying thought around with me. It accompanied me on my way to work and during my hard exercises at the gym. It was present as I tucked our girls into bed and as I slept next to my husband.

I realised Barack wanted to be president. I was convinced he'd be an excellent president. But, at the same time, I disliked political life. My employment was enjoyable. I was determined to give Sasha and Malia a stable and peaceful upbringing. I disliked interruption and uncertainty, and I knew a campaign would provide plenty of both. I knew we'd be subjecting ourselves to scrutiny. A great deal of scepticism. When you run for president, you are basically asking every American to vote for you or against you.

Let me tell you, that was terrifying.

I convinced myself that saying no would be a relief. Things would remain as they were if I answered no. We would stay in our house, in our city, in our existing occupations, surrounded by people we already knew. There would be no change in schools, no change in housing, and no other modifications.

And there it was, fully exposed, the thing my dread had been attempting to cover up: I didn't want to change. I didn't want to be uncomfortable, uncertain, or lose control. I didn't want my husband to run for president because I couldn't predict—or even imagine—what would come out of the experience. Of course, I had reasonable concerns, but what was I really terrified of? It was a novelty.

Recognizing this allowed me to think more clearly. It made the concept seem less absurd, less frightening. I was able to untangle my concerns in such a way that they no longer paralyzed me. I'd been doing this for years, dating back to my encounter with the turtle on Aunt Robbie's stage, and Barack had done the same. I reminded myself that the two of us had been through a lot of changes and new experiences in the past. We'd left the protection of our homes as teenagers to attend college. We'd both started new jobs. We'd gotten by as the only Black folks in a lot of places. Barack had previously won and lost elections. We'd suffered from infertility, the death of parents, and the stress of raising small children. Were we worried because of the uncertainties? Did the novelty make you feel uneasy? Yes, numerous times. And yet, hadn't we proven ourselves more capable, more adaptive along the way? We had. We were actually fairly skilled at it at this point.

When I start to hear the patter of negativity and self-criticism in my head, when my doubts begin to mount, I try to pause for a moment and name it as I see it. I've been trying to take a step back and approach my fear with familiarity, providing little more than a half-friendly shrug and a few simple words: Oh, hello. It's you once more.

Thank you for coming. For keeping me awake.

But I notice you.

You're not a monster in my eyes.

CHAPTER 3

Am I IMPORTANT?

By the time I reached high school, I was envious of the kids who could effortlessly fit in with the throng. Even though I was enjoying my classes and had a solid group of friends, I was still self-conscious about my height. I was aware of it almost all of the time. I was envious of the smaller girls, whose physical size didn't appear to influence how they dressed or whether any boy would think twice about asking them to dance.

Many of my leisure hours were spent looking for outfits that fit my shape and size. Most of the time, I had to settle for a less-than-ideal fit. I tried not to be discouraged as I watched my younger friends easily grab Calvin Klein jeans off the rack, not worrying for a second that the trouser legs might "flood." I agonised over heel heights, trying to seem hip but not overly tall. I was frequently distracted in class, tugging at the legs of my jeans, attempting to keep my ankles out of sight. And because the sleeves on my shirts and jackets were never long enough for my arms, I kept them rolled up all the time, thinking no one would notice. I expended a lot of energy hiding, changing, and compensating for what I wasn't. I continued attempting to squeeze myself into the spaces I was in. We were all trying to fit in. It's just part of being a teen, I've realised. It's what offers many of us our first exposure to failure. Even the popular, self-assured kids, I used to tell my daughters, are quietly terrified—just marginally better at concealing their own efforts to fit in. At that age, almost everyone is wearing a mask.

This type of self-consciousness is almost like a developmental stage—something to endure, learn from, and strive to overcome.

However, for many people, the sensation of not fitting in, of needing to exist outside of the norms that are presented to them, can last far into adulthood.

Do I have a place?

What do other people think of me?

How am I perceived?

We ask these questions and will occasionally bend ourselves to seek answers that don't hurt. To handle our differences in connection to the settings we find ourselves in, we adjust, hide, and compensate. We put on different masks—brave faces, really—for different settings in the hopes of feeling more safe or closer to a sense of belonging, but we never truly feel ourselves.

Nobody can make you feel awful about yourself if you feel good about yourself. It took me years to completely integrate my father's dictum into my own life. I gradually gained confidence, in fits and starts. Only gradually did I learn to embrace my uniqueness.

Whatever the signals were in those spaces—whether others perceived me as different, unqualified to be there, or problematic in some manner, even if what I was experiencing was unconscious or unintentional—I didn't need to allow those signals in. I had a choice in the matter. I could let my own life and actions speak for me. I could continue to show up and do the work. It wasn't my poison.

I discovered that I could feel better about my differences. It was useful to undertake a kind of psychological squaring of the shoulders while entering a new location. I could pause for a moment to remind myself of what I already knew to be true within the confines of my own home, within the safety of my friendships. My confirmation came from within. It also helps to be able to carry that strength into a different room.

I could rewrite the story of not-mattering in my thoughts, in real time, and for my own benefit: I'm tall, and that's a wonderful thing.

I'm a woman, which is a good thing.

I'm Black, which is a good thing.

I am myself, which is a good thing.

CHAPTER 4

GET ON WELL

When I married a man whose job required him to be away from home for days at a time, I was encouraged by my friends, especially those whose children enjoyed playing with mine. We became friends, carpooling to dance and swim lessons, feeding each other's children when someone had to stay late at work, and listening sympathetically if someone needed to vent, was hurting, or was attempting to make a major life decision. I had a few pals who, no matter how busy or crazy my own life felt, I'd gladly drop my own issues to help them with theirs. We covered for one another, making the ride more comfortable for everyone. The message among us was always, "I got you." I'll be present.

I've discovered that having close friendships helps to relieve stress in my marriage. Barack and I have never attempted to be each other's "everything" in life—to shoulder the complete load of care that each of us demands on our own. I don't expect him to want to hear every single one of my stories or thoughts, or to listen to every one of my worries, or to be exclusively responsible for my daily amusement and happiness. I also don't want to have to do all of the stuff for him. We instead distribute the load. Other types of emotional rescue and relief exist. We are carried by a diverse range of friendships—some his, some mine, and some ours together—and we do our best to assist in the carrying of our friends.

I believe I became more obsessive about my connections around the time I moved to Washington in early 2009, a time when I was feeling extremely pushed, depleting my own reserves of strength. Barack had been elected president, and within nine weeks, we'd packed our possessions in Chicago, taken Sasha and Malia out of school, and relocated to Washington, D.C., a city where I knew no one. We slept in a motel for the first few weeks before the inauguration, while the girls settled into their new school and Barack worked nonstop to put together his administration-in-waiting. I was making dozens of decisions every day about a future I couldn't fathom, from choosing which types of bedspreads and silverware to use in the White House to hiring employees for my East Wing offices. We were also planning to host roughly 150 personal visitors at the inauguration, including friends, relatives, and a large number of children, all of whom required itineraries, event tickets, and places to stay.

What I remember most about this period is the strange new gloss on everything, the impression that so much of our old life was being replaced so swiftly. We were in a new city, with many new people, new occupations, and a new life. My days became a bizarre mash-up of the everyday and the exceptional, the practical and the history. Sasha needed a pencil box, and I needed a ball gown. We required a toothbrush holder as well as a financial rescue package. I was also fast aware that we were going to need our pals.

Moving into the White House, I had this nagging fear that my friendships would never be the same, that all of the ties vital to our family would be altered as a result of the unusual pomp and grandeur that now surrounded us, the abrupt transformation in how we were perceived. I was concerned about how Sasha and Malia would interact with other children now that Secret Service personnel would be following them to every lesson, soccer practice, and birthday celebration. I wasn't sure how Barack would squeeze in a social life amid all of the crushingly pressing challenges he was dealing with. And I worried how, in the midst of all this increased commotion and security, I'd be able to keep my close pals near while still creating room for a few new ones.

I was not only new to Washington, a stranger among strangers, but I was also attempting to adjust to the fact that as First Lady, I'd become a target for others' attention. My presence in a room had the effect of changing the dynamics, not because of who I was, but because of what I was. As a result, I found myself becoming less interested in individuals who made a beeline for me and more intrigued in those who hung back.

My social worries were still largely on our girls at this moment. I was overjoyed when Sasha invited Olivia and a few of other girls over to spend a Saturday running around the house and then seeing a movie in the in-house cinema. I'd spent the morning pretending to do other things while discreetly lurking on the outskirts of their playdate, softly overtaken with emotion whenever a new peal of laughter emerged from Sasha's room. I felt a rush of relief after months of agonising over the intricacies of our transition to the White House. Friends were in the house, which was a sense of normalcy and a milestone event for our family.

When Barack was president, he was surrounded in the West Wing by fantastic colleagues—dialled-in, super-intelligent cabinet members and staffers who worked together to form a high-functioning team and an exceptional support system. But I witnessed firsthand the loneliness of the presidency—the enormous weight my husband bore as main decision maker, how the tensions piled up without release. He'd devote himself to dealing with one situation just to have another surface. He was frequently criticised for things he couldn't control, and he was sometimes chastised by people eager for change. He had to cope with a fractious Congress, a country reeling from the effects of the recession, and a slew of international concerns. I'd see him leave for his study after we'd finished dinner, knowing he'd be there until two a.m.—alone, awake, and trying to stay on top of it all.

He wasn't lonely per se—his life was far too busy for that—but he needed to get away. I was concerned about the job's arduous nature and what the stress may do to his health. I surprised Barack for his birthday a couple years into his presidency by inviting around 10 of his many friends to Camp David for a weekend of celebration and fun. It was the month of August. The United States Congress was not in session. He'd still be travelling with a slew of advisers and getting his daily briefings, but I believed he could at least try to unplug a little.

And he did unplug. I'm not sure I've ever seen anyone dive so fast into having fun as my husband did that weekend, which I took as a strong indicator of how badly he needed the break. His high school buddies had flown up from Hawaii, as had some college friends and some of his closest Chicago acquaintances. What exactly did they do? They had fun. While Sasha, Malia, and I, along with a few other wives and kids, sat out by the pool, the men immersed themselves in every activity Camp David had to offer.

It was as if they'd been granted a get-out-of-jail-free card that released them from their work and family commitments, and just like my pals and our Boot Camp weekends, they weren't going to waste a second of it. They engaged in basketball. They threw darts and played cards. They went skeet shooting. They played bowling. They held a home-run derby as well as a football throw. They kept track of everything, trash-talking their way through each tournament and discussing individual plays and upsets late into the night.

"Campathalon," as we began to call it, has become an institution in Barack's life, an annual gathering we now host on Martha's Vineyard, complete with prizes and an opening ceremony. For my diligent, sober-minded husband, it's a welcome respite, a return to the carefree days of childhood, a time to catch up with and be goofy with those he cares about. It's like a schoolyard recess, a chance for him to be free and a little wild while playing with his friends. It connects him to his happiness.

Life has taught me that strong friendships almost always result from strong intentions. Your table must be purposefully established, purposefully inhabited, and purposefully maintained. Not only should you tell someone you're curious about them, but you should also invest in that curiosity, setting aside time and energy for your friendship to grow and deepen, prioritising it over the things that will pile up and demand your attention in ways that friendship rarely does. I've discovered that creating rituals and routines around friendship—weekly coffees, monthly cocktails, annual gatherings—helps. Kathleen and I go for morning walks by the river on a regular basis. I belong to a group that has been organising an annual mother-daughter ski weekend for almost a decade, and the event is firmly entrenched in everyone's calendars and fiercely guarded, even by our kids, who now realise what having a Kitchen Table might mean in their own lives. My Boot Camp weekends have become less frequent and less intense than they once were, but I still enjoy sweating with you.

Researchers at the University of Virginia set out to investigate a particular notion regarding friendship. They attached heavy backpacks on a bunch of volunteers and lined them up in front of a large hill, as though they were about to climb it. Each volunteer was asked to estimate the slope. Half of them stood alone in front of the hill, while the other half stood beside someone they recognized as a friend. And those who were with a friend consistently saw the slope as less steep and the trek ahead as less tough. When long-time friends stood in front of the hill, the results were much more pronounced: the slope just seemed to flatten down more. This is the power of having others on your side. It's an excuse to look after your friends.

And that's what I'd like to tell everybody who is hesitant to enter into a new friendship or who is holding themselves back. It's what scares me when I hear from young people who are too afraid to take the chance or deal with the embarrassment of making new acquaintances. I want to remind kids that there is both richness and safety in other people if they are ready to stretch their curiosity in that way, if they can keep themselves open to it. Your circle of friends becomes your ecology. You are bringing more daisies into your life by making them. You are increasing the number of birds in the trees.

He wasn't lonely per se—his life was far too busy for that—but he needed to get away. I was concerned about the job's arduous nature and what the stress may do to his health. I surprised Barack for his birthday a couple years into his presidency by inviting around 10 of his many friends to Camp David for a weekend of celebration and fun. It was the month of August. The United States Congress was not in session. He'd still be travelling with a slew of advisers and getting his daily briefings, but I believed he could at least try to unplug a little.

And he did unplug. I'm not sure I've ever seen anyone dive so fast into having fun as my husband did that weekend, which I took as a strong indicator of how badly he needed the break. His high school buddies had flown up from Hawaii, as had some college friends and some of his closest Chicago acquaintances. What exactly did they do? They had fun. While Sasha, Malia, and I, along with a few other wives and kids, sat out by the pool, the men immersed themselves in every activity Camp David had to offer.

It was as if they'd been granted a get-out-of-jail-free card that released them from their work and family commitments, and just like my pals and our Boot Camp weekends, they weren't going to waste a second of it. They engaged in basketball. They threw darts and played cards. They went skeet shooting. They played bowling. They held a home-run derby as well as a football throw. They kept track of everything, trash-talking their way through each tournament and discussing individual plays and upsets late into the night.

"Campathalon," as we began to call it, has become an institution in Barack's life, an annual gathering we now host on Martha's Vineyard, complete with prizes and an opening ceremony. For my diligent, sober-minded husband, it's a welcome respite, a return to the carefree days of childhood, a time to catch up with and be goofy with those he cares about. It's like a schoolyard recess, a chance for him to be free and a little wild while playing with his friends. It connects him to his happiness.

CHAPTER 5

GOOD PARTNERSHIP

Our two girls shared an apartment in Los Angeles last year. They were both living in the city—Sasha at college, Malia in an entry-level writing job—and they'd gone out and selected a tiny house in a quiet neighbourhood that was convenient for both of them. The notion that they'd selected each other as housemates captivated me. It makes me happy to think that we raised siblings who are currently in their early twenties and are also friends.

The two of them moved into the unoccupied flat on the first day of the first month of their new lease. The majority of what they had appeared to be clothing. Our daughters, like many individuals their age, had been mostly itinerant up to that point, save for the months they were quarantined due to the virus. They'd bounced between college dorm rooms and furnished sublease flats, never bringing more than what might fit into a car trunk. A few times a year, one or both of them would return home for a week or two of vacation, swan-diving into the luxuries of our adult lives, rejoicing in the full fridge, the absence of roommates and easy access to laundry, and the loafing sweetness of a resident dog. They'd fill up on food, sleep, seclusion, and family time during these interludes. They'd then stash a few items in a closet, swapping out a set of winter clothes for a set of summer clothes or vice versa, and fly away like migratory birds.

But things are changing now. They'd found a more permanent home for themselves, something more permanent. Our daughters were becoming more mature, more firmly established in adulthood.

Over our video calls for the first month or two, I glimpsed glimpses of their home-decorating efforts. I'd notice a lovely new chair they'd gotten somewhere, or some framed images neatly displayed on the wall. They purchased a vacuum cleaner. They bought throw pillows, towels, and a set of steak knives, which I thought humorous given that neither of them was really fond of cooking or eating meat—or cooking in general. But the idea was that they were purposefully and proudly constructing a home. They were learning how to do "home" for themselves.

I was on FaceTime with Sasha one night when I was distracted by Malia, who was moving around in the background, running a Swiffer duster over a shelf full of trinkets and books. She was dusting their possessions! I couldn't help but note that she hadn't yet learnt to pick up or move the articles on the shelf so that they could be dusted on all sides.

But, hey, she was halfway through dusting! My heart felt like it was about to burst. Barack and I flew down to Los Angeles as quickly as we could. Sasha and Malia were overjoyed to show us around their new residence. They'd done a good job with it, having scoured yard sales and purchased at a neighbouring IKEA while keeping their budget in mind. They slept on box springs and mattresses with no bed frame, but they'd found some lovely bedspreads to cover it all. They'd found a set of unusual end tables at a flea market. They had a dining room table but had yet to find inexpensive seats.

We were all heading to a restaurant for supper, but they insisted on serving us a drink beforehand. As Barack and I sat on the couch, Malia pulled out a charcuterie board she'd assembled, declaring that she'd never realised how absurdly costly cheese can be.

"And I didn't even get any of the super-fancy ones!" she remarked.

Sasha made us a couple of weak martinis—Wait, you know how to make martinis?—and presented them in water glasses, first placing down a couple of newly acquired coasters so we wouldn't stain their brand-new coffee table. I was taken aback by everything that was going on. It's not that I'm startled that our children have grown up, but the entire scene—particularly the coasters—signalled a different kind of landmark, the type of thing that every parent spends years searching for, which is evidence of common sense. As Sasha laid our drinks down that night, I remembered all the coasters she and her sister hadn't bothered to use while in our care, all the times I'd tried to get water marks out of various tables, including the White House. However, the dynamics had shifted. We had arrived at their table. They owned it and were guarding it. They had clearly learned.

I'm cheering for my children to find their own path to maturity in their relationships, rather than focusing on the end outcome. I don't want kids to think of marriage as a prize to be pursued and won, or that a wedding is the kind of spectacle they need to properly launch a successful life, or that having children is ever a requirement. Instead, my hope is that kids will experience various levels of commitment, figuring out how to stop relationships that aren't working and how to begin new ones that appear promising. I want them to understand how to handle disagreements, the high sensations of closeness, and what it's like to have your heart shook. When and if my children finally pick someone to stay with for the rest of their lives, I want them to do so with confidence, knowing who they are and what they require.

I won't say anything else about my kids' romantic lives here out of respect for their privacy (and because they'd surely murder me). But I would add that it has been a joy to watch them practise and grow. What is my greatest want for them? I hope they find a place to call home, whatever that may be.

People frequently contact me for relationship advice. They comment on images of me and Barack together—the two of us laughing or sharing a gaze, appearing content to be side by side—and conclude that we like each other's company. They wonder how we've managed to stay married and miserable for thirty years. I'd like to remark, Yes, it truly surprises us at times! And I'm not even kidding. Of course, we have troubles, but I adore the man, and he loves me now, still, and seemingly forever.

Our love isn't flawless, but it's genuine, and we're dedicated to it. This particular certainty is parked in the middle of every room we enter, like a grand piano. My husband and I are extremely different people in many aspects. He's a night owl who prefers alone. I'm an early riser who enjoys a crowded environment. He spends far too much time golfing, in my opinion. In his opinion, I watch far too much lowbrow television. But there's a loving assurance between us that's as simple as knowing the other person will be there no matter what. That modest triumph we get to feel, knowing that despite having spent half our life together now, despite all the ways we irritate each other and all the ways we are different, neither of us has walked away, is what I believe others pick up on in those images. We are still present. We are still here.

I've lived in a lot of places during my adult life, but I've only ever had one true home. My family is my home. Barack is my name.

Our collaboration is something we developed together. We live in it every day, improving it as much as we can and sometimes letting it exist "as is" for long stretches when we're preoccupied with other things. Our marriage is where we take off and land, a place where we can each be completely, contentedly, and often irritatingly ourselves. We've learned to realise that this sphere we share, the energy and emotion between us, isn't always tidy and orderly, or exactly how one or both of us wants it, but the simple and reassuring fact is that it continues. It's become a firm piece of certainty for us in a world when certainty appears to be exceedingly difficult to come by.

A lot of the inquiries I get on social media or in letters and emails tend to revolve around the idea of certainty in relationships, how much of it we're expected to feel, when we're supposed to experience it, and with what level of strength and fluctuation. How do I know when I've discovered the ideal spouse, the type of person worth

23

committing to? Is it wrong for me to detest my partner at times? How do I do a good job of loving someone when my own parents set a poor example? What occurs when there is disagreement, annoyance, hardship, or a challenge?

I hear from people who are contemplating marriage and believe that being married will solve certain problems in their relationship. Or they're thinking about having a baby in the hopes that it will save their marriage. I occasionally hear from people who are contemplating divorce and are unsure whether to stay in or leave a relationship that is sour or difficult. Others tell me that marriage in general is a boring, patriarchal, and obsolete custom. And I hear from young people who are afraid of making mistakes in relationships, or who have already made mistakes and are unsure what to do next. "hey mrs michelle," a young woman called Lexi wrote me recently from Alabama, "i'm having a lot of boy problems..." From there, she poured her heart out.

The truth is that I don't have answers to these inquiries or prescriptions for anyone's unique problems. The only love tale I'm familiar with is the one I live inside every day. Your journey to certainty—if that's even what you're looking for—will differ from mine, just as your idea of home and who belongs there with you will always be unique to you.

Most of us only gradually discover what we need in intimate relationships and what we can contribute to them. We put in the time. We gain knowledge. We make mistakes. We occasionally acquire tools that do not genuinely serve us. Many of us make a few dubious investments early in our careers. For example, we might buy a bunch of steak knives, figuring that's what we're supposed to do.

We obsess, overthink, and waste energy. We may take incorrect advice or overlook good advice. When we are injured, we withdraw. When we are terrified, we arm ourselves. We may strike when provoked or concede when embarrassed. You could also decide, as many people do, that you are perfectly happy and fulfilled when you are not partnered up with anyone. And if this is the case, I hope you will recognize it for what it is: a perfectly valid and successful life choice. Many of us will unconsciously duplicate the connections we were brought in—whatever kind of home we knew as children—and this can, of course, work out brilliantly, horrifically, or somewhere in the between. I believe that true and lasting love occurs largely in the area of in-between. You are addressing the question, "Who are we and who do we want to be?" as a group.

I sometimes catch a glimpse of my hubby from a distance and feel as though I'm peeking through a time scrim. What I see is a grey-haired, slightly less scrawny, slightly more world-weary version of the twenty-seven-year-old guy who arrived as a summer associate at my corporate law firm decades ago, damp from a rainstorm, having travelled without an umbrella, and only slightly embarrassed for being late for his first day of work. What was it about his smile that made it so memorable? What was it about his voice that made it seem so good?

He was charming at the time. He is suddenly charming. He was a modest celebrity back then—a law student whose brilliance was causing a stir in legal circles—and he is, I assume, a major celebrity now. But, despite this, he's the same person, with the same elegance, the same heart and hang-ups, the same constant fight to be punctual or remember something as simple and functional as an umbrella on a wet day. He's the same oddball, alternately smooth and geeky person I met in the law firm's waiting room years ago, whose hand I shook and whose lanky height and unusual countenance I took in for the first time, not realising I was looking at my truest love and my life's greatest disrupter.

Like many others, I had preconceived notions about what marriage would be like, and just a few of them proved to be correct. My friends and I used to play fortune-telling games as kids, such as MASH, which predicted where we'd live, what kind of car we'd drive, and how many children we'd have, or another that involved folding up a piece of paper, origami-style, with hidden options for who we'd marry written beneath the flaps. We'd laugh and gasp at the varied outcomes: Would I actually marry Marlon Jackson of the Jackson 5 and live in California in a station wagon? Would my friend Terry really have nine children with our classmate Teddy and live in a Florida mansion?

What I did know was that the possibilities were huge and limitless. What I assumed would happen was a gorgeous wedding spectacle followed by years of scorching happiness and a passionate, never-settle-for-less way of life. Isn't that how it was intended to be? I was still too young to envision my own parents' marriage as something I'd want for myself one day. They were dedicated and friendly, conducting a useful and amicable cooperative operation regulated by common sense. They each made the other chuckle. They completed all of the jobs. Every year on Valentine's Day and my mother's birthday, my father would go over to the Evergreen Plaza shopping complex and buy her a new outfit, wrapping it in a bow and giving it to her.

I knew they were typically happy, but I had also seen a lot of All My Children, absorbing Erica Kane's famed hot-and-cold passions, which made my parents' marriage appear placid and dull. Instead, I allowed myself to conceive a fantasy-dream version of marriage and family life for myself, more akin to the dazzling romances my friends and I used to play out with our Barbies and Kens. I also understood from watching my grandparents that marriages did not always work out. My mother's parents had divorced long before I was born and, as far as I knew, had never spoken again. My father's parents had been estranged for most of his life but had, shockingly, reconciled.

I can see now that examples were all around me, indicating that long-term relationships are rarely flashy or seamless. My mother vividly remembers the first argument she ever had with my father, which happened shortly after their wedding in 1960, when she was twenty-three and he was twenty-five. They'd moved in together for the first time after a brief honeymoon and realised, rather abruptly, that they were entering this committed partnership with two sets of habits, two baked-in ways of doing things. What was the source of their first argument? It had nothing to do with money, having children, or anything else going on in the world at the time. It wasn't about which direction the toilet paper should hang on the roll in the bathroom, but about whether the loose end should be stretched over the top of the roll or fall beneath it.

Dad was reared in a "under" house, but Mom was raised in a "over" house, and the struggle felt epic and insurmountable for a time. With only two possibilities, one of them would have to concede and accept the other's method. A disagreement may appear small, but what is behind it is often not. When you merge your life with someone else's, you are immediately confronted with—and frequently required to conform to—the history and patterns of behaviour of another family. In the instance of the Great Toilet Paper Dispute of 1960, it was my mother who eventually resigned, concluding it was far too silly for anyone to be arguing about. She simply chose to disregard it. Following that, our family lived peacefully as an "under" family. The subject was never brought up again, at least not until Craig and I had grown up and found our own partners. (As it turns out, the Obamas are "over" people, and they remain so to this day.) This type of high-stakes/low-stakes negotiation is common in marriage.

In Becoming, I wrote about how, despite their typically stable relationship, my mother used to consider leaving my father. She'd conduct a type of mental exercise every now and again, allowing herself to imagine what might happen if she chose to walk out the door on Euclid Avenue and find herself in a different life, with a different man, in a different place. What if the outcome of her origami fortune-telling game had been different? What if she'd married a millionaire, a mystery man from the South, or a boy she'd known since junior high?

She generally allowed herself these ideas in the spring after another ice cold winter, another season of dark days spent mostly indoors in our small little room. The Difference sounded appealing at the time. The Difference was like the fresh air flowing in through the windows once it warmed up enough to open them again. Different was an engrossing fantasy, a fictitious honeymoon in her imagination.

And then she'd giggle to herself, picturing what kind of new hell a strange man from the South would have wreaked in her life, knowing that the kid from junior high had his own pile of messes, and that any millionaire would undoubtedly show up with a slew of problems. And then the phoney honeymoon would be over, and she'd be back to real life, back to my father. It was, I believe, her way of slowly renewing something in her heart, recalling the nice and caring home she had, her reasons to stay.

You will live by your decision to try to establish a life with another individual. You'll have to make the decision to stay rather than run over and over again. It helps to enter a committed relationship prepared to work, ready to be humbled, and willing to tolerate and even enjoy living in that in-between area, bouncing between the poles of beautiful and dreadful, sometimes in a single discussion, sometimes over the course of years. And inside that decision and those years, you will almost probably discover that there is no such thing as a fifty-fifty balance. Instead, it'll be like abacus beads moving back and forth, with the maths rarely tidy and the problem never entirely answered. A dynamic relationship is one that is always changing and evolving. At no moment will you both feel that everything is absolutely fair and equal. Someone will always be making adjustments. Someone will always make a sacrifice. One person may be on top while the other is on the bottom; one may endure more financial burdens while the other handles caring and family commitments. Those options, as well as the stresses that come with them, are real. But I've come to learn that life happens in seasons. Your happiness—in love, family, and career—rarely comes at once. In a healthy partnership, both people will take turns compromising, creating that shared sense of home in the in-between.

Regardless of how wild and profoundly in love you are, you will be required to accept many of your partner's flaws. You'll have to ignore all sorts of tiny annoyances, as well as a few significant ones, in order to express love and constancy above everything—over all the bumps and inevitable disruptions. You will need to do this as frequently and gently as possible. And you'll need to do it with someone who is equally capable and willing to create the same latitude and show the same patience toward you—to love you despite all of your baggage, despite what you look like and how you behave when you're at your very worst.

When you think about it, it's an absurd and seemingly against-the-odds proposition. And it isn't always effective. (It should not always work: if you are being injured in a relationship, it is time to end it.) But when it works, it may feel like a genuine miracle, which is what love is after all. That is the entire point. Any long-term connection is, in essence, an act of unwavering faith.

When Barack and I decided to start a family, it wasn't because we had a set of promises. I couldn't really predict how anything would turn out. We weren't financially comfortable yet; we both had years of student loans to pay off. On any front, there were no predictable outcomes. In fact, I married him knowing he was a server, someone who would always—predictably!—take the less-certain path to fulfilment. You could count on him to reject any sort of conventional path and to question everything that came too readily. He was committed to juggling multiple professions, turning down lucrative corporate positions in order to create books, educate, and stay true to his ideals. Neither of us had any family fortune to rely on. We quickly discovered that even our capacity to have children was a question mark, kicking off a difficult few years of fertility issues. There was also his political career's crazy, flying motorcycle ride. We went into all that craziness together, knowing of only one thing: we'd be better off facing it as a group.

I learned early on that a relationship is not a solution to your problems or a substitute for your wants. People are who they are; you can't make them become someone they don't want to be or someone they've never seen modelled for them. I desired a mate who was guided by his own values and not by my affection. I desired someone who was truthful because he respected truthfulness, and faithful because he cherished fidelity.

I tell my daughters now: You don't want to settle down with someone because you're searching for a breadwinner, a carer, a parent for your children, or a way out of your troubles. In my experience, such arrangements rarely work out well. Instead, the idea is to identify someone who will work alongside you rather than for you, contributing on all fronts and in all ways. When someone declares that they only want to play one role, such as "I make the money, so don't expect me to change diapers," my advice is to start running for the hills. I tell my girls that a good partnership is like a winning basketball team, consisting of two skilled individuals with fully developed and transferable skill sets. Each player must be able to dribble, pass, and defend in addition to shooting.

That doesn't imply you won't adjust for one other's flaws or differences. It's only that you'll have to cover the entire court together while remaining versatile throughout time. A partnership does not change who you are, even if it challenges you to be more accepting of the demands of others. I, like Barack, haven't changed much in the thirty-three years since we met. I'm still the same reasonable striver who shook his hand the first time, and he's still the scholarly optimist who thinks on three levels at once.

The difference is in what's between us, the million subtle adjustments, compromises, and sacrifices we've each made to accommodate the other's intimate presence, this hybrid energy of him and me together—us two—now seasoned and battle-tested over decades. Whatever modest stirring occurred between us on that first day of our acquaintance, whatever seed of mutual curiosity was sown at the moment we shook hands and began to talk, is what has developed and ripened into certainty over time. That is the continual wonder, the ongoing discussion, the house in which we dwell. He is himself. I'm me. It's just that we've gotten to know each other. Really, really, really, really well.

I've always tried to help people see beyond the sparkly side of my life with Barack and into our true selves. I've made a concerted effort to dispel the myths that my husband is a great man, that our marriage is ideal, and that love in general is a carefree affair. I've previously written about how Barack and I sought—and urgently needed—couples counselling when we began to become prickly and distant with one another when our children were little and we were both exhausted. I've joked about all the times I was so fed up with my husband that I wanted to throw him out the window, all the minor resentments I'm capable of harbouring, even now, probably forever. True intimacy may be vexing. Nonetheless, we remain.

Despite the fact that I've spoken frequently and openly about our unpolished areas, others appear to prefer the façade. A New York Times columnist once chastised me for mentioning that my husband was not a deity, but rather a person who occasionally forgets to pick his socks up off the floor or put the butter back in the fridge. My own opinion on this stays unaltered, and I believe it is true for individuals in general: we only injure ourselves when we hide our genuine selves.

Carissa, a friend of mine, recently spent more than a year avoiding a lot of reality with a man she was dating. Carissa is a beautiful African American woman in her thirties who runs her own business, has many friends, and is a successful person by many standards. The only problem was that she disliked being alone. She desired a companion. She hoped to have children one day. She'd met this guy online and really liked him. They began to go out. They had a fantastic time on their quick excursion to the Caribbean. They returned home and continued to see each other, despite the fact that they were both preoccupied with their work and their own circle of friends. Carissa explained that they were "keeping it casual."

What she didn't recognize at the time was that she and this man were effectively repeating the same first date, denying any desire to develop emotionally closer. They were trapped inside "casual," having fun, but never risking something as simple as a minor argument or a probing conversation, something that may break either of them open or necessitate further investigation. Casual was supposed to imply simple. Being together was supposed to be free of all work and hardship. The point is, the "real" always appears. It will eventually track you down.

Carissa asked both her man and one of her closest girlfriends to dinner one evening at her apartment more than a year into their relationship, introducing them for the first time. Throughout the meal, she observed as her normally outgoing buddy innocently prodded the guy with genuine questions, almost methodically exposing all sorts of things that Carissa was completely unfamiliar with. It turned out that he had a strained relationship with his father. As a child, he had felt unloved. In previous relationships, he had struggled to commit.

None of this seemed very troubling. It was all fresh, a side of this person Carissa had never seen before. She realised she'd been too terrified to go looking for it. She'd never asked him many questions, and he'd never asked her anything deep or personal about herself. They'd been hooking up while avoiding emotional closeness for months, each striving to remain invulnerable. Carissa had convinced herself that she could handle "casual," even if it contradicted her own life aspirations. And did he really want to be casual? She was completely unaware. They'd never actually talked about any of it in depth. It felt too late to begin. It was as if they'd spent the previous year eating candy instead of meals.

Carissa realised she'd concealed herself behind a mask, pretending she wasn't craving for more or better, all the while believing that the passage of time counted as development in the relationship. She later informed me that she had held back from exhibiting too much inquiry or asking about commitment because she was afraid it would make her appear "high-maintenance" and thus radioactive. She might be ambitious in her career and meticulous in her daily life, but when it came to being with a man, she believed those same qualities would work against her. Carissa hadn't wanted to appear to be eager to put effort into a relationship because she was afraid it would make her undeserving of additional attention from a person she didn't even know. "I didn't want to seem thirsty or needy," she explained. "I was just trying to play it cool." But, in the end, keeping her calm had gotten her—and them—nowhere.

I occasionally speak with young people who have created an art of embracing the casual and playing it cool, oblivious to the fact that being honest and vulnerable is a pillar of true connection. They haven't realised that there is room for depth and authenticity in relationships, even during the flea-market stage of life. They may spend their twenties hooking up but not learning the fundamentals of commitment and good communication, the idea that it is possible to communicate genuine sentiments and vulnerabilities. They consume a lot of sugar yet gain no muscle. When it comes time to go serious, when they envision a family life and a more settled existence, they are suddenly, and often frantically, learning these skills for the first time, recognizing that there is little casual or cool about a long-term commitment.

What struck me about Barack immediately away was his lack of interest in being casual. His candour with me was, at first, a little shocking. Prior to meeting him, I had met men who were unsure of themselves and their desires. I'd gone out with a couple of players— guys who were attractive and fascinating to be around, but who were constantly peeking over my shoulder, trying to see who else was in the room, what other connections could be formed. My first romances taught me the same lessons as everybody else's: I'd been cheated on and lied to on several occasions. This was during my own flea-market time of life, when I was experimenting with many ways of being and preparing myself for the life to come. In those early partnerships, I was unsure. I could be ambiguous. I was still figuring myself out, trying to make sense of my own needs and desires.

Barack was unlike anyone I'd ever met before. He was upfront and obvious about what he wanted, and his assurance was unique, at least when it came to me. I probably wouldn't have noticed how strange it was if I hadn't already had a few practice relationships.

"I like you," he said several weeks later, after we'd met and gone out for a few professional lunches. "I believe we should begin dating." I'd be delighted to take you out."

Even while I debated whether to give in to my increasing feelings for him, worried about the propriety of an office romance, Barack remained unflappable and quietly persistent, certain we were a good match. He gave me time to think about it, but he made it apparent that I was interesting to him, that he liked being around me, and that he wanted more. He expressed himself in much the same way I'd see him do years later in the Oval Office, tenting his fingers together and putting out his thoughts like a sequence of well-reasoned bullet points:

First and foremost, he felt I was gorgeous and intelligent. Second, he assumed I liked chatting to him as well. Third, because he was only a summer hire, he would hardly qualify as an office romance.

Number four, he only wanted to spend time with me. And, given that he'd be back at law school in about eight weeks, we didn't have much time. So, what's the harm? There would be no typical cat-and-mouse love gamesmanship with him. He was uninterested in tinkering. Instead, he eliminated all uncertainty. He placed his feelings on the table and then walked away, as if to say, "Here's my interest." Here's my admiration. This is where I'll begin. From here, we can only move forward. This combination of openness and assurance was, I must say, charming and refreshing. It was also quite sensual. Oahu appeared wonderful and just as I'd imagined it from the plane window, the reality flowing over the illusion in a near-perfect overlay. On a late-December afternoon as we circled Honolulu, I had Barack next to me and paradise down below. I could see the Pacific's gleaming blue waves, lush green volcanic mountains, and the curving white arc of Waikiki Beach. I couldn't believe it was happening to me.

We took a taxi from the airport to the apartment complex on South Beretania Street where Barack had grown up with his grandparents while his mother was away doing anthropological fieldwork in Indonesia. On that car ride, I was impressed by how startlingly enormous and urban Honolulu appeared to be, a metropolis built close to a body of water similar to Chicago. There was a freeway, traffic, and skyscrapers, none of which I remembered seeing during the Brady Bunch's visit and none of which had entered my daydreams. My mind was racing, collecting everything in and processing it like data. I was twenty-five years old and seeing this location for the first time, along with this guy I thought I knew but didn't really understand, trying to make sense of it all. We drove by a series of densely packed high-rise apartment complexes, whose balconies were crowded with bikes and potted plants, and people's laundry was strung up and drying in the sun. Oh, right, this is real life, I recall thinking.

Barack's grandparents lived in a high-rise, though not a particularly large one. It was blocky and modernist, fashioned of functional concrete. An old church with a large green lawn stood across the street. We took the elevator to the tenth floor, lugging our bags through the humid air along an outdoor hallway on the building's exterior until, finally, after many hours of travel, we arrived at the entrance to their apartment, the home Barack had lived in for the longest time.

35

I'd met Barack's mother, his grandparents (Toot and Gramps), and his younger sister, Maya, who was nineteen at the time. (I'd meet the Kenyan side of his family a year or so later, including his sister Auma, with whom he'd grown very close.) They were friendly and curious about me, but most of all, they appeared ecstatic to have Barack—"Bar," as they called him (short for Barry and pronounced "Bear") back in the house.

I spent the following 10 days getting to know Honolulu and Barack's family. He and I remained in the basement of an apartment owned by one of Maya's acquaintances. We would go hand in hand over to the high-rise on South Beretania and stay for a couple of hours, conversing while everyone worked on a jigsaw puzzle or sat outside on the small lanai that overlooked the church across the street. The apartment was small and comfortable, with a combination of Indonesian batiks and Midwestern items that reminded me of Dandy and Grandma's old Chicago apartment. When I first saw Barack's house, one of the first things that struck me was that he'd grown up in similar conditions to mine. Toot served tuna sandwiches topped with French's mustard and sweet pickles, much like we'd enjoyed at home on Euclid Avenue, on TV trays in the living room.

Barack and I were both unique and similar. Everything was clearer to me now. I saw the gaps between what was familiar and what was unfamiliar as he reconnected with his family after a year apart.

Barack and his mother reunited by engaging in lengthy discussions about geopolitics and the situation of the globe. Gramps, on the other hand, enjoyed making people laugh. Toot, who had retired from a bank position a few years before, was suffering from back discomfort, which made her a little grumpy, but she enjoyed playing cards. She was no-nonsense, I could tell, having borne the brunt of the burden of sustaining the entire family for many years. Maya was

encouraged to utter every thought in my head. My family was never short on time. When my head implodes at the start of a fight, the last thing I want to do is engage in some instantaneously reasonable, bullet-pointed conversation about who's right or what the solution is. It turns out that when I'm trapped, I'm capable of saying some stupid, nasty things. In our relationship, Barack has pushed for an immediate conversation and promptly gotten scorched by the steam of my rage.

We've had to figure it out on our own. We've had to practise responding to one other in ways that take both of our experiences, needs, and ways of being into account. Barack has learned how to give me more room and time to calm down and process my feelings gradually, knowing that I was raised with that kind of space and time. I've also learnt how to be more efficient and less harmful while processing. And, knowing that he was raised not to let things fester, I strive not to let them linger for too long.

We discovered that there is no right or wrong way to proceed. We don't follow any rigid set of cooperation principles. There is only what we, two extremely distinct persons, can work out between us, day by day and year by year, via pushing and yielding, drawing from deep wells of patience as we try to understand each other a bit more. I prefer actual presence to words. I value punctuality, time commitment, routine, and consistency—all of which were less important in his upbringing. Barack emphasises having space to think, resisting any type of establishment, and living simply and with a high degree of flexibility—all of which were less essential in the home I grew up in. It always helps to be able to acknowledge our emotions and locate some of our disagreements within our personal background rather than blaming others.

Barack and I would leave his grandparents' apartment in the afternoons and walk several miles to the quieter side of Waikiki Beach, stopping at a convenience shop for food along the way. We'd pick an open location near the ocean and set out a rattan mat on the sand. It was at these moments that I felt we were finally on vacation, away from both job and home, fully present with each other. We'd swim in the ocean and then lie out in the sun to dry off, talking for hours on end, until suddenly, Barack would stand up, towel the sand off his body, and say, "Well, we've got to get back."

Oh, okay, I'd think, a little disappointed. This is everyday life.

The truth is that all I desired at the time was a fantasy version of Hawaii. Rather than schlepping the few miles back to South Beretania Street for a no-frills dinner with the grandparents in front of the evening news, rather than watching Barack stay up late helping Maya figure out her tuition payment plan or talking with his mother about her perpetually-behind-schedule doctoral dissertation about the economics of blacksmithing in rural Indonesia, I would have loved to sat, just the two of us, unhitched from all obligations Finally, I would have loved to have stumbled off a bit giddy to some top-floor honeymoon suite in a hotel.

That's how I'd imagined Hawaii back in my office in Chicago, as I'd submitted my request to take these valuable vacation days off work. That was all I could think about as Barack rolled up the rattan mat and we began the long trip back. I was still young, you see. In my thoughts, I had a balance sheet with my gains on one side and my sacrifices on the other. But I didn't know what was actually valuable. I was still piecing together what I'd need for the coming years and life, what would keep my heart racing for the long haul. It is not mai tais or honeymoon suites, I can assure you. It is not beautiful sunsets in exotic locations, or having a lavish wedding, or having money, or keeping a glittering presence in the world. It is none of those things.

It took me a while to grasp what I was seeing. It took 10 straight evenings in that modest high-rise apartment on South Beretania Street for me to completely realise what I was seeing, and what a gain on my own bank sheet it would eventually become. I was with a man who was committed to his family and went back every morning and night, knowing it would be a year before he could return. The way his sky was organised reminded me of his version of consistency. Later, after we'd moved in together, I realised that even when they were physically separated, Barack remained at the centre of his family, filling a role that neither of his mother's husbands had ever filled, attentively counselling Ann and Maya through various crises, problem-solving with them over the phone whenever problems arose.

The fact that I'd witnessed all of this would aid us during the worst period of our marriage, when our girls were still small and Barack was spending three or four nights away from home each week to fulfil his job as a politician. I'd been raised with a different type of consistency and closeness, and his absence left me feeling vulnerable and shaky, a little abandoned. I was concerned that there was a chasm between us that would become too large to bridge.

But once we were able to talk about it, especially with the support of a counsellor, we were reminded of what we already had, the platform. I was familiar with Barack's narrative, and he was familiar with mine. It helped us comprehend that we would endure the gaps as long as we were aware of them. We may reside somewhere in the middle. We both knew that distance was something he was used to, even if it wasn't something I was. Even though he was far away, he knew how to love. He'd had no choice but to do it his entire life. The daughters and I would always be at the centre of his universe. I'd never be left behind. On that first trip, he'd revealed it to me.

Night after night in our Honolulu apartment, I'd watched Barack clear and scrape the dinner plates, do the crossword puzzle with his grandfather, recommend books to his sister, and read all the fine print on his mother's financial statements to make sure she wasn't getting ripped off. He was focused, patient, and present. He wouldn't go until the day was over, the dishes were done, the talks were all over, and everyone was yawning.

I may have wished for the honeymoon suite and this man's undivided attention, but he was instead allowing me to see the real, showing me some version of how our own future may unfold if we chose to. We weren't casual, and we weren't trying to be cool, which is how I realised we'd wind up being far more than just visitors in one other's lives. This is when conviction begins, late one night in an elevator on your way down from the tenth level. As you step out into the warm Honolulu night with a dome of stars overhead, you are struck by the unexpected feeling that you have arrived home.

Every year, Barack and I travel to Hawaii together. We always return at Christmastime to meet our grown-up daughters, both of whom have just returned from their own homes and lives. We get together with Barack's sister, Maya, and her family, see old high school friends, and host various mainland friends. After more than thirty years of visiting Oahu, I no longer gasp when I see the wafting palm trees out the plane window or am as taken aback by the sight of Diamond Head, the giant green barrier southeast of Waikiki.

What I'm experiencing right now is the exhilaration of familiarity. I'm drawn to this location in ways I never envisioned for myself as a child. Though I am only a guest, I am quite familiar with this one island, as well as the man who introduced me to it through our regular and consistent visits. I swear I know every turn on the roadway that connects the airport to the North Shore. I know where to go for great shaved ice and Korean BBQ. I can smell plumeria in the air and enjoy the underwater shadow of a manta ray thrashing its way across shallow water. I'm familiar with the calm waters of Hanauma Bay, where we taught our toddlers to swim, and the windswept sea cliffs of Lanai Lookout, where my husband visits to mourn his adored mother and grandmother, whose ashes he scattered there.

Barack and I travelled to Honolulu to celebrate our wedding anniversary a few years ago, and he surprised me with a celebration meal in the town. He'd reserved a private area on the rooftop terrace of an oceanfront hotel and hired a small band to perform. We stood for a long time, taking in the scenery. It was late afternoon, and we could see the full length of Waikiki Beach. Surfers floated lazily on their boards, waiting for the right wave, and old men played chess in the park below. We could see the zoo, where we used to take our girls on our yearly Christmas trips, and the hustle and bustle of Kalakaua Avenue, where we'd often wander with them at night to watch the jugglers and other sidewalk performers who amused tourists. We pointed out the many hotels we'd stayed in throughout the years, once we'd saved up enough money to stop relying on Barack's family to get us a borrowed room, recognizing that we were staring out at the span of all the years we'd now spent returning to this spot together. It felt like coming full circle. My childish fantasy of visiting Hawaii had come true. I was alone on a rooftop at sunset with the person I loved. Barack and I sat down and ordered a couple of martinis. We talked about his family for a while, recalling our first visit to South Beretania Street and how young we'd both been—how, in retrospect, it seemed like we'd barely known each other at all. We remembered the rattan mat and all those long trips to the beach and back to his grandparents' house. We laughed, realising it had been a long day. We clink our glasses and watch the sky turn pink.

Marian Robinson, my 71-year-old mother, was planning to relocate to the White House with us after Barack was elected president. The plan was for her to assist in the care of Sasha and Malia, who were seven and ten years old at the time. She'd make sure everyone was okay and then return to Chicago. The media became enamoured with this idea right once, asking interviews with my mother and generating a spate of pieces dubbed "First Granny" and "Grandmother-in-Chief." It was as if a new and possibly interesting character had been cast in a network program. My mum was suddenly in the news. She made headlines.

If you've ever met my mother, you'll know that being well-known is the last thing she wants. She consented to do a few interviews, assuming it was just part of the wider transition process, but she repeatedly expressed astonishment that anyone would care. My mother is ordinary by her own standards. She also likes to claim that, while she adores us, my brother and I are not exceptional. We're just two kids who got a lot of love and a lot of luck and ended up doing well. She wants to remind people that places like Chicago's South Side are teeming with "little Michelles and little Craigs." They're in every school and on every street. It's just that far too many of them are neglected and underrated, resulting in far too much unrealized potential. This is arguably the cornerstone of my mother's bigger philosophy: "All children are great children."

My mum is now 85 years old. She moves with a gentle and amusing ease. Glamour and gravitas are irrelevant to her. She sees right through it, believing that everyone deserves to be treated equally. I've seen her speak to both the Pope and the Postman, approaching both with the same calm, unflappable tone. If someone asks her a question, she responds in simple and direct language, with an amused detachment and never tailoring her answers to a specific audience. Another characteristic of my mother is that she does not believe in embellishing the facts.

As we moved into the White House, this meant that if a reporter asked my mother a question, she would answer it truthfully rather than soft-pedalling her ideas or according to any set of talking points created by frightened communications employees. No, we quickly realised that if Grandma was going to go to the media, she was going to speak her truth and get it over with.

That's how she made national headlines, detailing how she'd been dragged kicking and screaming from her quiet little cottage on Euclid Avenue and more or less forced to reside at the nation's most famous address by her own children. She wasn't being ungracious; she was simply being honest. My mother expressed herself to the reporters in the same manner that she had expressed herself to me. (The postman and the Pope would have both heard the same thing.) She had refused to come to Washington, but I had begged her. When begging didn't work, I recruited Craig's help to further twist her arm. My mother was our family's rock. She kept us all in check. She'd been helping us out around the edges of our regular childcare arrangements since our daughters were babies, filling the gaps as Barack and I frequently improvised and occasionally flailed our way through different career transitions, heavy workload cycles, and the ever-expanding after-school lives of our two young girls. So, sure, I did coerce her into coming.

CHAPTER 6

PARTNERING WELL

Marian Robinson, my 71-year-old mother, was planning to relocate to the White House with us after Barack was elected president. The plan was for her to assist in the care of Sasha and Malia, who were seven and ten years old at the time. She'd make sure everyone was okay and then return to Chicago. The media became enamoured with this idea right once, asking interviews with my mother and generating a spate of pieces dubbed "First Granny" and "Grandmother-in-Chief." It was as if a new and possibly interesting character had been cast in a network program. My mum was suddenly in the news. She made headlines.

If you've ever met my mother, you'll know that being well-known is the last thing she wants. She consented to do a few interviews, assuming it was just part of the wider transition process, but she repeatedly expressed astonishment that anyone would care.

My mother is ordinary by her own standards. She also likes to claim that, while she adores us, my brother and I are not exceptional. We're just two kids who got a lot of love and a lot of luck and ended up doing well. She wants to remind people that places like Chicago's South Side are teeming with "little Michelles and little Craigs." They're in every school and on every street. It's just that far too many of them are neglected and underrated, resulting in far too much unrealized potential. This is arguably the cornerstone of my mother's bigger philosophy: "All children are great children."

My mum is now 85 years old. She moves with a gentle and amusing ease. Glamour and gravitas are irrelevant to her. She sees right through it, believing that everyone deserves to be treated equally. I've seen her speak to both the Pope and the Postman, approaching both with the same calm, unflappable tone. If someone asks her a question, she responds in simple and direct language, with an amused detachment and never tailoring her answers to a specific audience. Another characteristic of my mother is that she does not believe in embellishing the facts.

As we moved into the White House, this meant that if a reporter asked my mother a question, she would answer it truthfully rather than soft-pedalling her ideas or according to any set of talking points created by frightened communications employees. No, we quickly realised that if Grandma was going to go to the media, she was going to speak her truth and get it over with.

That's how she made national headlines, detailing how she'd been dragged kicking and screaming from her quiet little cottage on Euclid Avenue and more or less forced to reside at the nation's most famous address by her own children.

She wasn't being ungracious; she was simply being honest. My mother expressed herself to the reporters in the same manner that she had expressed herself to me. (The postman and the Pope would have both heard the same thing.) She had refused to come to Washington, but I had begged her. When begging didn't work, I recruited Craig's help to further twist her arm. My mother was our family's rock. She kept us all in check. She'd been helping us out around the edges of our regular childcare arrangements since our daughters were babies, filling the gaps as Barack and I frequently improvised and occasionally flailed our way through different career transitions, heavy workload cycles, and the ever-expanding after-school lives of our two young girls. So, sure, I did coerce her into coming.

The issue was that she was happy at home. She'd just retired from her work. She preferred her own existence in her own space and was averse to change in general. Her valuables were all in the house on Euclid. It had the bed she'd slept on for over three decades. Her impression was that the White House felt more like a museum than a home. (Of course, she made her statement in front of a reporter.) Even as she stated that her move to Washington was mainly uninvited and intended to be temporary, she maintained that her love for Sasha and Malia, her devotion to their growth and well-being, ultimately trumped all else. "If anyone else is going to be with these kids other than their parents," she shrugged to a reporter.

After that, she declared she was done with interviews. My mother became quite popular in the White House after she moved there, even though she didn't set out to be. She truly became the belle of the ball. Everyone simply called her "Mrs. R." People on staff liked her since she was so low-key. The butlers, who were largely Black, appreciated having a Black grandmother around. They showed her pictures of their own grandchildren and occasionally sought her counsel on life. When the White House florists came to change the floral arrangements, they would stop to visit with my mother. On days when she strolled through the gates and headed to the CVS on Fourteenth Street, or over to Filene's Basement in the opposite direction, or when she dropped by Betty Currie's house—Betty being Bill Clinton's former secretary—to play cards, Secret Service personnel kept eyes on her. The housekeepers on staff were always attempting to persuade my mother to let them do more for her, even though Mom was adamant that no one should wait on or clean up after her when she knew quite well how to do it herself.

"Just show me how to use the washing machine and I'll be fine," she explained.

We attempted to keep her chores light because we were aware of the favour she was doing us. She accompanied Sasha and Malia to and from school, assisting them in adjusting to their new routine. She made sure the girls had food and whatever else they needed for after-school activities on days when I was occupied with FLOTUS duties. She listened intently to their stories about what had happened during the day, just as she did when I was in elementary school. When she and I had time alone, she'd fill me in on whatever I'd missed during the day with the kids, and then she'd do the same for me, acting as my sponge and sounding board.

My mother kept herself hidden when she wasn't caring after the girls. Her belief was that we should have our own family lives, separate from hers. And she believed that she, too, should have a life apart from us. She enjoyed her independence. She appreciated her personal space. She tended to be hands-off as a general rule. She had come to D.C. with only one goal in mind: to be a dependable support to Barack and me, as well as a caring grandma to our two children. Everything else, in her opinion, was simply fuss and noise.

We would occasionally host VIP guests for dinner parties in the White House residence. They'd look around and wonder where my mother was, if she'd be joining us for dinner.

I'd generally simply chuckle and gesture up to the third floor, where she had a bedroom and preferred to hang out in an adjacent sitting room with enormous windows overlooking the Washington Monument. "Nope," I'd reply, "Grandma's upstairs in her happy place."

This was effectively code for, "Sorry, Bono, Mom's got a glass of wine on her TV tray, some pork ribs on her TV tray, and Jeopardy! is on." Don't even think you'll be able to compete..." Overall, the agreement appeared to be successful. My mother ended up remaining in the White House with us for the entire eight years. The stability of her presence, her low-key, low-drama approach to life, benefited us all, especially since so much around Barack's job was high-key and high-drama. Grandma kept us on track. She wasn't there to monitor what was going on with Ebola, the filibuster, or who was causing havoc by flying test ballistic missiles over the Sea of Japan.

She was only there to keep a loose tab on how our family was doing. And we were in desperate need of it. We required her. She was our anchor. Over the course of eight years, our children grew from wide-eyed elementary schoolers to blossoming teenagers keen on gaining independence and adult privileges. They tested some boundaries and did some stupid things, as teens do. Someone was grounded for failing to observe curfew. Someone submitted an odd bikini selfie on Instagram, and the East Wing communications team immediately told them to take it down. Secret Service officers once had to pull someone from an uncontrolled high school party just before local law police arrived. Someone reacted angrily when the president of the United States asked (undiplomatically) how she could study Spanish while listening to rap.

Even minor disobedience or misconduct from our adolescent kids would send a wave of uneasy worry through me. It preyed on my worst fear: that life in the White House was ruining our children. Which is, of course, their parents' fault. In these moments, my old companion, the scared mind, would go into overdrive, causing a chain reaction of doubt and shame. (Did I mention the fearful mentality adores children? It is aware of all your weak points and will target them accordingly.)

My mother-guilt would come in when just one small thing went wrong. I'd start questioning every decision Barack and I had ever made, every fork in the path we'd ever taken. As we've discussed, women are programmed to thrive at self-scrutiny, having been put into systems of inequity and fed completely unrealistic notions of female "perfection" since we were children. None of us—absolutely none—ever measure up. Nonetheless, we persevere. The fantasy versions of being a parent, like marriage and partnership, live at the forefront of our cultural imagination, although the reality is far, far, far less perfect.

Feelings of inadequacy can be especially poignant for mothers. The images of maternal perfection we see in advertising and on social media are frequently no less perplexing or fabricated than the enhanced and manipulated female bodies—starved, sculpted, and pumped with fillers—that are so often held up as the societal gold standard for beauty. But we are still conditioned to believe it, striving for not only the perfect body, but also perfect children, perfect work-life balances, perfect family experiences, and perfect levels of patience and serenity, despite the reality that none of us—truly none—will ever live up to it. The mistrust created by all of this deception can be powerful and destabilising. As a mother, it's difficult not to wonder, "Is everyone else doing this perfectly except me?"

I am just as prone to self-laceration as the next individual. At the first sign of conflict or difficulty with our children, I would immediately and viciously begin searching for my own errors. Had I been too harsh or too indulgent with them? Was I overly present or underutilised? Was there any parenting book I'd neglected to read fifteen years before? Was this a genuine crisis, or a harbinger of deeper problems? Which crucial life lessons had I overlooked? Was it now too late?

If you have any responsibility for a child's life, you are surely familiar with this particular brand of fear and worry, the sleep-stealing agony of worrying about your kids—that haunting, lost-in-the-woods feeling that you have somehow not done enough for them, or that you've done everything wrong, and they are now paying the price for your negligence or poor decision-making. It's something I believe many of us feel profoundly and almost incessantly, beginning with those first moments when we take in the sweet and innocent perfection of a small newborn face and think: Please, oh please, don't let me mess you up.

As a parent, you are always fighting your own desperation not to fail at your job. From baby brain gyms and ergonomic strollers to SAT instructors, entire industries have been developed to feed and benefit on this desperation. It's like a gap that will never be filled. And while many parents in the United States struggle with the exorbitant cost of daycare (which can take up to 20% of the average worker's wage), the pressures mount. You may become convinced that if you take even a small step back, because of one insignificant benefit you didn't figure out how to supply or afford, you've potentially doomed your own child.

I'm sorry to announce that this does not stop with a single milestone. When your child learns to sleep or walk, or starts kindergarten, or graduates from high school, or even moves into their first apartment and gets a set of steak knives, the desperation does not go away. You will continue to be concerned! You'll still be scared for them! You'll be wondering if there's anything else you can do as long as you're still breathing. When you have a child, even an adult, wandering about in the world, it becomes exponentially more dark and dangerous. And most of us will go to great lengths to convince ourselves that we have even a semblance of control. Even now, my husband, the former commander in chief, can't stop texting our daughters warnings about the hazards of highway driving or wandering alone at night. He emailed them a lengthy essay about earthquake preparedness and offered to have the Secret Service give them a natural-disaster-response briefing when they relocated to California. (This was received with a respectful "No, thanks." Caring for your children and watching them grow is one of the most rewarding tasks on the planet, but it can also drive you insane.

But, over the years, I've had one secret weapon to help stop the flood of parental anxiety: my own mother. She's been my saviour, my Buddha, a nonjudgmental observer of my flaws and, as such, a necessary source of sanity. My mother has kept a close eye on our daughters' growth and development for the entirety of their early lives, never interfering with the decisions Barack and I have made along the way.

She provides perspective and presence. She is an attentive listener, someone who can quickly push my fear to the back of the room or reign me in when I'm going "extra" with my worrying. She advises me to always assume the best in children, that it is preferable to let

52

them live up to your expectations and high esteem rather than expecting them to live down to your fears and worries. My mother believes that rather than making children earn your trust, you should give it to them. This is her take on "starting kind." Throughout my time in the White House, Mom was there to provide me with on-the-spot reality checks. She'd reflect Sasha and Malia's adolescence back to me with the unblinking eyes of a septuagenarian, reminding me that whatever was going on was developmentally appropriate and within the realm of expectation—and that I'd done some of the same dumb things myself. Her pep talks were brief and subtle, which suited her personality, but they were also reassuring. "Those girls are alright," my mother would say, shrugging. "They're just trying to learn life." What she meant was that I, too, was fine, that I could relax and trust my own judgement. This has always been central to my mother's message.

If you spend enough time with my mother, you will realise that she is prone to sprinkling such little pearls of wisdom into ordinary discourse. They are usually linked to her idea that it is possible to raise respectful children without drama or fuss. These are never blustering declarations delivered with venom or zeal. You practically have to bend in close and listen for them instead. They are usually witty comments that slip out discreetly, almost like stray pennies from her pocket.

For years, I've been collecting these pennies, stuffing them into my own pockets and utilising them as a guide and a tool to offset my own doubts and fears as a parent. For a while, I considered having my mother write her own book, in which she might recount her life story and share some of the ideas that I have found to be so helpful. When I suggested it, she just shrugged and said, "Now, why on earth would I do that?"

She has, however, granted me permission to share a few of her tried-and-true maxims here, some of the points she's made that have helped me become a bit calmer, slightly less guilt-ridden, slightly more good mom to my own children. But only if I include this warning from my mother: "Just make sure they know I'm not in the business of telling anybody how to live."

1. Teach your children to wake up on their own.

My parents gave me a little electric alarm clock when I was five years old and started kindergarten. It had a square face with small green glow-in-the-dark hands pointing to the hour and minute. My mother demonstrated how to set my alarm and turn it off when it buzzed. She then assisted me in working backward through all of the things I'd need to do in the morning—eat breakfast, brush my hair and teeth, pick out my clothes, tie my shoes, and so on—to determine how long it would take me to get myself up and out the door to school. She was there to teach me, and she'd given me the tool, but it was up to me to figure out how to use it properly.

And I just adored the alarm clock. I adored what it provided me: power and control over my own tiny life. My mother, I realise now, had given me this weapon at a carefully chosen time in my development, before I was old enough to be cynical about having to get up for school in the morning, before she'd ever have to start shaking me up personally. It saved her some trouble, but the real gift was to me: I could wake myself up. I could jolt myself up!

My mother was not interested in nagging or cajoling me if I ever slept through my alarm or otherwise was sluggish and dragged my feet about going to school. She kept her distance, making it apparent that my life was mostly mine. "Listen, I got my education," she'd tell you. "I already went to school." It's not about me."

2. It's not all about you. Good parents are constantly attempting to put their children out of business.

The alarm-clock strategy was part of an even more deliberate effort on my parents' side to teach us kids how to get on our feet and stay on our feet, not only physically but emotionally. My mother had one objective in mind since the day she gave birth to each of her children: to make herself more or less obsolete in our lives. Given

55

that I've just completed expressing how much I've needed my mother's calming presence in recent years, it's evident she has a long way to go. But it's not for a want of effort.

My mother made no bones about the fact that her objective was to become as unimportant in our lives as possible, as quickly as possible, especially when it came to day-to-day practical responsibilities. The sooner that day came, and she believed Craig and I could handle our own affairs, the more successful she'd consider herself to be as a parent. "I'm not raising babies," she would say. "I am responsible for raising adults."

It may sound scandalous to say, especially in this day and age when helicopter parenting is the norm, but I'm pretty sure most of my mother's decisions were led by one simple question: What's the least I can do for them right now?

This was not a careless or self-serving inquiry, but rather one that was profoundly considered. Self-sufficiency was paramount in our household. My parents recognized that they were working with a limited budget—of money, space, access to privilege, and, in the case of my father's health, not just energy but time remaining on earth—which drove them to be frugal on all fronts. My father believed that we were fortunate and that we should never take any of that good fortune for granted. We were taught to enjoy what was in front of us, whether it was a bowl of ice cream or the opportunity to go to the circus. He urged us to enjoy the moment we were in, to resist the need to hunt for the next indulgence or thrill, or to envy what others had.

"Never satisfied!" he'd exclaim lightly if someone ripped open a birthday gift and then hurriedly looked for the next. If we asked for a second helping of ice cream before the first was finished, he'd say, "Never satisfied!" He challenged us to think about our desires.

Our parents' main contribution was to teach us to rely on ourselves and to think clearly about what we needed. They couldn't give us shortcuts, so they focused on teaching us skills. Their hopes for their children were encapsulated in one single thought: If Craig and I were to travel further in life than they had, we would want large engines and full tanks of fuel, not to mention the capacity to conduct our own repairs.

My mother believed that her hands merely got in the way of ours. If we needed to learn something new, she'd show us how to do it and then immediately stand aside. Craig and I learned to wash and dry dishes with the help of a step stool long before we were tall enough to reach the sink. As a matter of habit, we were obliged to make our own beds and wash our own laundry. As I previously stated, Mom encouraged me to walk to and from school on my own, allowing me to discover my own way. All of these were minor abilities, but they represented daily experience in self-reliance and problem-solving, a step-by-step overcoming of doubt and fear, until there was less overall to question and fear. Exploration and discovery became easier. We were able to establish many habits from one stable habit.

We accomplished a lot of this stuff imperfectly, but the idea was that we did it. Nobody was doing anything for us. My mum was not going to intervene. She didn't correct our mistakes or put a stop to our method of doing things, even if it differed slightly from hers. This, I believe, was my first experience with power. I appreciated being trusted to complete a task. "It's easier for kids to make mistakes when they're little," my mother recently told me when I asked her about it. "Leave it to them to make them." You also can't make too big of a thing out of it. Because if you do, they'll give up."

She stood back and let us struggle and make mistakes with our chores, homework, and relationships with various teachers, coaches, and friends. None of it was motivated by her own self-esteem or ego, nor was it done for the sake of bragging rights. She'd swear it wasn't about her at all. After all, she was trying to wash her hands of us.

This meant that her mood was unaffected by our successes. Her pleasure was not determined by whether we received A's on our report cards, if Craig scored a lot of points in his basketball game, or whether I was chosen to the student council. She was glad for us when good things happened. When unpleasant things happened, she would assist us in processing them before returning to her own tasks and challenges. The main thing was that she loved us whether we succeeded or not. She smiled every time we went through the door.

My mother kept a silent eye on what was going on in our lives, but she did not immediately offer to fight our conflicts. Much of what we were learning was social, gaining abilities to identify who we wanted to be with, whose voices we allowed into our thoughts, and why. She made time to volunteer in our classrooms at school when she could, which offered her a useful window into our daily lives and undoubtedly helped her distinguish when we actually needed help versus when we were just "learning life," which appeared to be most of the time.

My mom would stand in the kitchen and listen to whatever tirade I had to unleash about the unfairness of some teacher's remark, or the stupidity of an assignment, or how Mrs. So-and-So clearly didn't know what she was doing on days when I came home stewing about something a teacher had done (and I'll admit, this happened with some regularity).

And after I was finished, when the steam of my rage had subsided enough for me to think straight, she'd pose a simple question—one that was both genuine and a little bit leading. "Do you need me to go there for you?"

I did, however, require my mother's assistance on a few occasions over the years, and I received it. But I didn't need her to step in on my behalf 99 percent of the time. She was discreetly pushing me to continue figuring through the situation in my thoughts just by asking that question and giving me a chance to react. How horrible was it in reality? What were the remedies? What could I possibly do?

This is how I typically knew I could rely on my own response, which was "I think I can handle it." My mother helped me figure out my own sentiments and ways for dealing with them, largely by giving them space and not smothering them with her own thoughts or opinions. If I got too upset about something, she'd instruct me to go perform one of my tasks, not as punishment, but as a way of resolving the issue. "Get up and clean that bathroom," mom would tell me. "It will divert your attention away from yourself."

She created a type of emotional sandbox inside our small house where Craig and I could safely rehearse our feelings and sort through our reactions to whatever was going on in our young lives. She listened as we worked out our difficulties aloud, whether it was a maths problem or a playground problem. When she gave counsel, it was usually of the hard-boiled and practical sort. Most of the time, it was a reminder to preserve perspective and to think backward from the desired outcome—to constantly be focused on that.

My mum once heard my complaint about having to cope with an arrogant maths teacher while I was in high school, nodded understandingly, and then shrugged. "You don't have to like your teacher, and she doesn't have to like you," she pointed out. "But she's got the maths in her head that you need in yours, so maybe you should just go to school and get the maths." She grinned at me, as if this were the easiest thing in the world to understand. "You can come home if you want to be liked," she explained. "We will always like you here."

3. Recognize what is actually valuable.

My mother recalls a large coffee table in the centre of the living room made of smooth, fragile glass in the house she grew up in on the South Side. Because it was breakable, everyone in the family had to go around it on tiptoe.

My mother was a keen observer of her own family. She was seated directly in the middle of seven children, giving her plenty to observe. She had three elder siblings and three younger siblings, as well as two parents who appeared to be polar opposites and had little in common. She had spent years absorbing the dynamics around her, quietly and possibly unknowingly constructing her notions about how she would raise her own family eventually.

She observed how her father, my grandpa Southside, cared for his children, particularly her three older sisters. Fearful of what was beyond his control, he drove them about in his car so they wouldn't have to ride the bus. He awakened them up in the mornings, eliminating the need for them to set an alarm. He seems to cherish their reliance on him.

My mother took notice. Meanwhile, my mother's mother, Rebecca, was stiff and proper, clearly unhappy, and likely clinically depressed (as my mother now believes). She wanted to be a nurse when she was younger, but her mother, a washerwoman who raised seven children in Virginia and North Carolina, supposedly informed her that nursing school was expensive and that Black nurses rarely obtained good jobs. So Rebecca married my grandfather and had seven children instead, never seeming to be happy with the outcome of her life. (She'd also eventually become dissatisfied enough to leave, moving out when my mother was approximately fourteen and supporting herself as a nursing aide. Without her, Southside ran a more casual household.)

Grandmother Rebecca's house had a rule that children should be seen rather than heard. My mother and her siblings were taught to be silent at the dinner table, to listen mutely and respectfully to the adult talk around them, never contributing to it themselves. My mother recalls vividly the sensation of having a slew of unspoken thoughts accumulating in her mind. It was unsettling. It did not sit well with her. Even psychologically, they were all treading carefully, watching where and how they walked.

When her mother's friends came to visit, my mother and her siblings were expected to sit in the living room with the adults. From babies to teenagers, they were all supposed to sit nicely at the perimeter, saying little more than hello. My mother recalls spending many evenings in that room with her mouth clenched shut in anguish, hearing enough adult-speak she wanted to engage with, lots of ideas she wanted to debate or at least better understand. She spent hours attempting to keep her thoughts to herself, all the while staring at that glass coffee table, which was always spotless and sparkling, with not a single smudge or fingerprint on it. It must have been during these hours that my mother, unwittingly, came to the realisation that her own children would one day be not just allowed but encouraged to speak. This will become the established doctrine on Euclid Avenue years later. Every thought was welcome, and every viewpoint was cherished. No sincere question would ever be denied. Laughter and tears were allowed. Nobody would have to walk on tiptoe.

My mother recalls a new visitor scrutinising all the little faces and restless bodies crammed into the living room and finally posing a logical question: "How could you possibly have a glass table like this and all of these kids?" My mother doesn't remember how my grandma reacted, but she knew in her heart what the true answer was: Her own mother, in her eyes, had missed an important lesson about what was valuable and what was not. What was the use of seeing children if you couldn't hear them? No youngster in her household would ever dare to touch that glass table, just as no one would dare to talk if they knew they'd be punished for even trying. They were being restrained rather than allowed to grow. Finally, when my mother was around twelve years old, some grown-up friends came over to their house to visit, and for some inexplicable reason, one of them decided to sit down on the table. It burst into bits on the floor, much to my grandmother's horror, and as her children watched solemnly. It felt like cosmic justice to Mom. This anecdote still makes her laugh to this day.

4. Take care of the child you have.

Nothing approaching a glass table could be found in the flat where my parents reared us. We didn't have much in our lives that was delicate or breakable. True, we couldn't afford anything extravagant, but in the aftermath of her own upbringing, my mother had no desire to buy showpieces of any kind. She'd never pretend that anything beneath our roof was more valuable than our bodies and spirits.

Craig and I were allowed to be ourselves at home. Craig was a natural caregiver as well as a bit of a worrier. I was fiery and self-sufficient. Our parents regarded us as individuals and treated us accordingly. They aimed their parenting towards developing our individual qualities and bringing out the best in us, rather than trying to shoehorn us into a predetermined pattern. My brother and I were respectful of our elders and followed some fundamental norms, but we also argued at the dinner table, threw balls inside, listened to music on the stereo, and horsed around on the couch. When something broke—a water glass, a coffee mug, or, every now and then, a window—it wasn't a big concern.

I tried to apply the similar technique to Sasha and Malia's upbringing. I wanted children to feel seen and heard—to constantly express themselves, to explore freely, and to never feel the need to tread carefully in their own house. Barack and I set the following ground rules and guiding principles for our household: I, like my mother, insisted on our children making their beds as soon as they were old enough to sleep in them. Like his mother, Barack was all about getting the girls involved in the pleasures of books as early as possible.

What we immediately discovered, however, was that rearing little children followed the same basic pattern as pregnancy and childbirth: You can spend a lot of time thinking, preparing, and arranging for family life to go smoothly, but in the end, you're left to deal with whatever happens. You may create systems and routines, and choose from a dizzying array of sleep, feeding, and discipline gurus. You can write your family bylaws and express your faith and philosophy aloud, and you can go on and on about it with your partner. But sooner or later, you'll be brought to your knees, understanding that despite your best and most genuine efforts, you're only marginally—and often very marginally—in control. You may have spent years captaining your own ocean liner with exemplary command and pristine levels of cleanliness and order, but now you must face the fact that there are pint-sized hijackers on board, and they're going to smash the place up whether you like it or not.

Your children, as much as they adore you, have their own agendas. They are individuals who will acquire lessons in their own unique way, regardless of how thoroughly you plan them. They are bursting with eagerness to investigate, test, and touch what is around them. They will breach your ship's bridge, place their hands on every surface, and accidentally shatter everything fragile, including your patience.

Here's one I'm not very proud of. It happened one evening when Malia was around seven years old and Sasha was only four years old, when we were still living in Chicago. After a tough day at work, I arrived home. As was typically the case back then, Barack was in Washington, D.C., in the midst of a Senate session that I was undoubtedly resentful of. I'd given the kids supper, asked how their days had gone, supervised bath time, and was now sagging a little on my feet, wanting to be off duty and find even a half-hour to sit quietly by myself.

The children were meant to be brushing their teeth before bed, but I could hear them giggling furiously as they ran up and down the stairs to our third-floor playroom. "Hey, Malia, Sasha, it's time to wind down!" From the bottom of the stairs, I cried out. "Now!" There was a little pause—maybe three seconds—before more thunderous footsteps and another cry of laughter. "It's past time to settle down!" I yelled once more. Nonetheless, it was evident that I was shouting into the vacuum, completely ignored by my own children. I could feel the heat rising in my cheeks, my patience eroding, my steam rising, and my stack threatening to blow.

All I wanted in the world was for those youngsters to go to sleep. My mother had always told me as a child to try to count to ten in these situations, to halt just long enough to latch onto some reason—to respond rather than react. I got as far as counting to eight before I couldn't take it any longer. I was done. And I was enraged. I dashed up the stairs, yelling for the girls to come out of the playroom and join me on the landing. I then took a deep breath and counted the last two seconds of my wrath. When the girls appeared, flushed and a touch sweaty from the fun they'd been having, and completely unaffected by all the commands I'd been shouting up the stairs, I told them I quit. I was leaving my position as their mother.

I mustered what little control I could get and exclaimed, not very calmly, "Look, you don't listen to me." You appear to believe that you do not require a mother. You seem perfectly content to be in charge of yourself, so go ahead....From now on, you can feed and dress yourself. And then you can go to sleep. I'm giving you your own tiny lives, which you can handle on your own. "I don't mind." I threw my hands in the air, demonstrating how helpless and hurt I was. "I am done," I declared. It was at this point that I got one of the clearest glimpses of who I was dealing with in my life. Malia's eyes widened, and her lower lip began to shake. "Oh, Mommy," she expressed concern, "I don't want that to happen." And she dashed straight to the bathroom to clean her teeth.

Something in me softened. That worked quickly, I thought. Meanwhile, four-year-old Sasha stood clutching the little blue blanket she liked to carry around, taking a second to comprehend the news of my departure before expressing her own emotional reaction, which was pure and unconstrained relief. After her sister had gone out obediently, Sasha turned without saying anything and scampered back upstairs to the playroom, as if to say, Finally! This lady is none of my concern! I heard her turn on the television within seconds.

I'd given that child the keys to her own life in a fit of exhaustion and irritation, and it turned out she was more than glad to accept them long before she was ready. As much as I enjoyed my mother's idea of ultimately becoming obsolete in my children's lives, it was far too early to call it quits. (I quickly summoned Sasha from the playroom, marched her through tooth brushing, and tucked her into bed.)

This one episode taught me an essential lesson about how to raise my children. I had one who wanted more and one who wanted fewer guardrails from her parents, one who would react to my emotions first and another who would take my words at face value. Each child has her own temperament, sensitivities, needs, abilities, set of boundaries, and methods of understanding her surroundings. As our children developed, Barack and I saw these same dynamics play out again and again. Malia tended to execute controlled, precise turns on the ski slopes, but Sasha preferred to bomb straight downhill with her jacket billowing. If you asked Sasha about her day at school, she'd respond with five words before bounding off to her bedroom, whereas Malia would give you a full account of every hour she'd been gone. Malia frequently sought our advice—like her father, she liked to make decisions methodically and with input—whereas Sasha thrived when we trusted her to do her own thing, just as I did as a child. Neither was correct or incorrect, good or evil. They were and continue to be distinct.

As a mother, I learned to depend less on parenting books and well-meaning advice givers and more on my own instincts, recalling my own mother's timeless counsel to "calm down and trust my judgement." Barack and I gradually started to read our own children for signs, adapting to what they were each showing us and attempting to understand their growth through what we knew about their distinct gifts and needs. I began to think of parenting as an art form, similar to fly-fishing, in which you stand for hours knee-deep in a swirling river, trying to calculate not only the water current but also the movement of the wind and the position of the sun, a practice in which your best manoeuvres are executed only through delicate flicks of the wrist. Your patience, perspective, and precision are all important.

In the end, your child will mature into the person they were born to be. They will experience life in their own unique way. You will have some say in how things go for them, but not all of them. Unhappiness cannot be removed from their life. You will not be able to eliminate conflict. What you can give your children—what we can all give children—is the opportunity to be heard and seen, the practice they need to make rational decisions based on significant values, and the consistency of your gratitude that they are present.

5. Return home. We'll always like you around here.

This was something my mum frequently told me and Craig. It was the statement that stood out above all others. You arrived home hoping to be liked. Home was a place where you could always find joy. I've written a lot about the concept of home in these chapters. I recognize that I was fortunate to have met an excellent one early on. As a child, I was able to soak in joy, which provided me a significant advantage as I grew and developed as a person. Knowing what it felt like to be glad, I was able to go out and seek more of it, to seek friends and relationships, and eventually a partner who helped bring even more light, more gladness, into my world—which I then attempted to pour into the lives of my own children, hoping to offer them the same boost. Finding and appreciating the light inside other people has become arguably my most significant weapon for overcoming uncertainty and dealing with adversity, seeing through thickets of cynicism and despair, and, most importantly, maintaining my hopefulness.

I understand that "home" can be a more confusing and uncomfortable concept for many people. It could represent a location, a group of people, or a type of emotional experience that you are attempting to overcome. Home may be a painful place to which you never want to return. And that's fine. Knowing where you don't want to go gives you power.

Then there's the power of figuring out where you want to go next. How do we create spaces where joy thrives—for ourselves, for others, and especially for children—and where we will always want to return? You may need to bravely reinvent your concept of home, scraping together a shelter for yourself, nurturing the parts of your flame that may have gone unnoticed or unkindled when you were a child. It is possible that you may need to build a chosen family rather than a biological one, safeguarding the boundaries that keep you safe. Some of us may have to make drastic adjustments in our lives, rebuilding and repopulating our spaces several times before we understand what it means to be accepted, supported, and loved.

My mother relocated to Washington with us (again, kicking and screaming), partly to help with our children, but also because I needed her approval. I am nothing more than a grown-up child, someone who comes through the door at the end of a hard day, exhausted and a little needy, searching for solace, acceptance, and maybe a snack.

My mum raised us all in her wise and straightforward manner. Every day, she lit up for us so that we may light up for others. She was instrumental in making the White House feel less like a museum and more like a home. During those eight years, Barack and I attempted to invite more people, of all races and origins, and especially children, into that house, urging them to touch the furniture and investigate what was there. We believed students could connect with history while also recognizing that they mattered enough—that they were valuable enough—to determine its future. We wanted it to seem like a palace of joy, powered by a sense of belonging and conveying one simple, powerful message: You will always be welcome here.

Of course, Mom will take no credit for any of it. She'll be the first to tell you—even now—that she's nothing remarkable, and it's never been about her. My mother enthusiastically packed her bags late in 2016, approximately a month before a new president was sworn in. There was little fanfare and, at her request, no departure party. She just left the White House and returned to Chicago, to her old apartment on Euclid Avenue, to her old bed and old stuff, relieved that she'd finished the job.

CHAPTER 7

THE WHOLE OF US

I occasionally read profiles of high-earning, successful women who claim to have and do it all. They give off an effortless vibe—well-groomed, well-dressed, and excellent at running whatever empire they happen to run, while also appearing to make dinner for their kids at night, fold every piece of laundry in the house, and still have time for yoga and weekend trips to the farmers market. We occasionally get ideas on how they do it, such as time management tactics or life hacks involving mascara, or which incense to burn or what to put in an acai smoothie. All of this is presented alongside a list of five super-literary novels that they have recently finished reading.

I'm here to inform you it's a little more complicated than that. Most of the time, what you see in those profiles is a person sitting on top of a metaphorical pyramid, looking graceful, balanced, and in command. But, first and foremost, any balance is likely to be transient. Second, it is only because of the collaborative efforts of a team that frequently includes managers, childcare workers, housekeepers, hair stylists, and other professionals who have dedicated themselves to that person's efficiency and care. Many of us, including me, rely on the quiet and often unnoticed work of others. Nobody achieves success on their own. I believe it is critical for those of us who have had behind-the-scenes assistance to make a point of mentioning it as part of our story.

If you know me, you'll recognize the extraordinarily skilled and level-headed individuals who have served on my team throughout the years. They are the issue solvers, the detail trackers, the boosters of my own efficiency and capacity to function. During my time in the White House, I was aided by two dynamic young women, Kristin Jarvis during the first term and Kristin Jones during the second, who were at my side for practically every step I took in public, helping to keep me moving forward and prepared for whatever came next. They are still like big sisters to Sasha and Malia.

Since leaving the White House, I've worked on a range of new projects, including authoring books, executive producing television series, and assisting with the management of the Obama Foundation, all while continuing to advocate for issues like voting rights, girls' education, and children's health. Melissa Winter, who left a job on Capitol Hill in 2007 to assist me during Barack's presidential campaign, then became an important deputy in the East Wing, and is still with me fifteen years later, now holding the position of chief of staff, expertly running my office and managing a wide range of responsibilities across every aspect of my professional life. It's difficult to overestimate how much I rely on her.

I was fortunate to have a tremendously skilled assistant called Chynna Clayton join my East Wing staff in 2015 and then agree to stay on with me as I transitioned into life as a private citizen for the first five years after leaving the White House. Chynna was my air traffic controller, my day-to-day, moment-to-moment life coordinator. When a friend asked if I was available for dinner the next Tuesday, I'd generally laugh and respond, "You gotta ask my mom." Mom is, of course, Chynna, and Chynna is in charge of the calendar.

Chynna managed to keep my credit cards. My mother's phone number was in her possession. She spoke with my doctors, planned my trips, worked with my Secret Service detail, and organised my excursions with friends. She could adjust to any situation and stay unflappable in the face of change. On any given day, I could be talking with a group of students at a school, filming a television show, or recording a podcast. I might meet with a world leader or the head of a charitable organisation before dining with A-list celebrities. Every move was facilitated by Chynna.

We were basically always together because of her employment. We drove together in the automobile. On the plane, we sat next to one other. We stayed in adjoining rooms in hotels. We were close because of the distance we travelled. When we lost our dear old dog Bo, Chynna wept with me. I rejoiced alongside her when she purchased her first home. Chynna became not just a part of my life, but also a close friend.

That's why I was surprised when Chynna requested if the two of us could have a formal, one-on-one meeting around a year after we left the White House. Given how much time we'd already spent together, it was an odd request, and Chynna sounded apprehensive when she made it, throwing me into a tailspin of my own. I assumed the meeting meant one thing: she was going to inform me she was leaving.

I braced myself for the news as Chynna entered my office and took a seat.

"Uh, ma'am?" she inquired. (Calling me "ma'am" is an odd leftover from my days in the White House, a habit of deference that a number of our longtime colleagues insist on maintaining.) "I'd like to tell you something..."

"Okay, I'm listening."

"Well, it's really about my family."

I noticed her shifting nervously in her seat. "All right," I replied.

"Specifically about my father."

"Go on..."

"I guess I've never mentioned it, but I feel like I should." He was imprisoned."

"Oh, Chynna," I said, assuming that was recent news. I knew Doris King, Chynna's mother, but I'd never met her father, nor had she told me anything about him. "That sounds harsh. I'm truly sorry. "When did this occur?"

"Well, he got locked up when I was three."

I waited for a second, mentally performing the arithmetic. "You mean he went to prison twenty-five years ago?"

"Yeah, something along those lines. He escaped when I was thirteen." She gave me a perplexed expression. "I just thought you should know in case there was a problem."

"Is there a problem?" "How could that be a problem?"

"I'm not sure. I was just concerned that it might be."

"Wait," I advised. "Have you been worried about this the whole time you've worked for me?"

Her smile was soft and bashful. "Only a little. Yes."

"And that's why you wanted to have this meeting?"

Chynna gave a nod.

"So, you're not quitting?"

She was taken aback by the suggestion. "What? No."

We stared at each other for a few seconds before falling silent, I believe due to mutual relief.

I finally began to laugh. "You know, you almost killed me with that one," I pointed out. "I thought you were leaving." "No, ma'am, not at all." Chynna was giggling as well. "I just needed to tell you that one thing." It felt like the right time." We sat and chatted for a while after that, both of us realising how important "that one thing" was.

Telling that part of her tale was a kind of unburdening for Chynna, a letting go of something she'd been hanging onto for a long time. She told me that she had been ashamed to tell others about her father's incarceration her entire life. She'd kept it hidden from her instructors and friends when she was younger because she didn't want to be judged or stereotyped because of how her family was structured or what they were going through. She'd felt the stakes increasing as she went on to college and then started working among a lot of presumably fancy people at the White House, the chasm between her childhood circumstances and where she now found herself growing larger. How can you casually explain to your Air Force One seatmate that as a child, you'd only seen your father during visits to a federal penitentiary?

It had become a matter of habit and strategy for her to leave that aspect of her story out. And yet, the effort it sometimes required for her to skirt around it, to avoid engaging in any conversation that would lead her back to her past, had conditioned her to feel guarded and careful, as if she were wearing an extra coat of armour. She'd been living quietly, terrified that she'd be exposed as a fraud. Of course, she wasn't.

That day in my office, I couldn't tell Chynna enough how much her story—her entire story—was fine with me. I was relieved to learn this. It simply increased my regard for her, giving me a better understanding of the incredibly competent young woman who sat before me. The fact that she had effectively weathered the burden of having a parent in prison throughout her childhood demonstrated her resilience, independence, and perseverance. It provided insight into how she'd become such a whiz at problem-solving and logistics, having learnt to think swiftly and on various levels at a young age. Her inability to decide what to do with that part of her tale may have also explained why she had remained one of our staff's more reserved members. I wasn't just gazing at one aspect of this person I suddenly admired, but at all of her—or at least more of her. I was seeing someone whose life has several chapters.

I knew Chynna grew up in Miami, raised by a devoted mother who'd done the job of parenting alone, working the graveyard shift to be present for her daughter after school, encouraging her to take every opportunity. I'd met Doris a few times over the years and witnessed firsthand how proud she was of her daughter. Chynna's route, career, intelligence, and maturity were all triumphs. Her achievement was due in part to her mother's investment and hard work.

I also knew from my own childhood that this kind of support may often translate into more pressure, even if your loved ones don't mean it that way. When you're the first in your family to leave your neighbourhood, the first to go to college, the first to own a house or gain any sort of foothold into stability, you carry the pride and expectations of everyone who came before you, everyone who waved you toward the mountaintop, trusting that you'd get there even if they couldn't.

As beautiful as this is, it also becomes something additional to carry, something important that you can't afford to be careless about. You leave your house knowing you're carrying a platter piled high with the hopes and sacrifices of others. And now you're balancing that tray on a tightrope while navigating school and job contexts where you're perceived as different and your belonging is never guaranteed.

You may be forgiven for not wanting to risk more by exposing so much of your personal tale in the midst of all that effort and peril. You may be excused for your inwardness, prudence, and layers of armour. All you're actually trying to do is concentrate, stay balanced, and not fall.

Chynna now described our chat as helping to release something in her, allowing her to shed some of that dread and let go of the feeling she was an impostor in her own professional life. She opted to let a particular part of herself out of the vault and into the light, a bit of her history that had always made her feel vulnerable, a piece of her despite, inside the protection of our close relationship, the trust we'd developed over time.

I understand why sharing was risky for her, despite the fact that the two of us had a considerably more personal and close relationship than most people had with their bosses. And I know that in many settings, or for someone fresher to her position, or if Chynna had been more isolated as a woman or person of colour on our team, this type of danger would have felt even more significant. What we reveal in professional situations, what we exhibit of ourselves and when, is not only personal but also inherently complicated—a frequently delicate question of timing, context, and careful judgement. We must always be aware of what is at stake and who will be receiving our truth. There is no such thing as a universal rule of thumb.

In the next chapters, we'll go over when and how to share yourself in honest and successful ways. But first, let me explain why I believe it is crucial that we seek out these opportunities to become more comfortable with ourselves and our experiences, as well as to provide space and acceptance for the stories of others—whether at work or in our personal life, or, in an ideal world, both.

On the most basic level, it can be liberating to take a calculated risk and let something out of the vault, freeing yourself from the duty to keep it hidden or from attempting to compensate for whatever distinguishes you from your peers. It frequently indicates that you are beginning to incorporate the aspects of yourself that have been left out into your wider idea of self-worth. It's a way of finding your own light, which often helps others see theirs as well. For some, this can be a very private process, carried through with the assistance of a counsellor and discussed only within the most secure of relationships. It can take years for the ideal timing and collection of circumstances to present themselves. Many of us wait far too long before even attempting to understand or give voice to our own tales. What matters most is that we discover ways to analyse what's in the vault and consider whether or not keeping it inside serves us.

Chynna says she started to feel more confident and comfortable speaking about this part of her story with others in her life after telling me more about her upbringing and realising that it didn't change my high regard for her, prompting her to fear a little less and feel more confident and comfortable in general. She also realised how much of her energy had gone unwittingly into the withholding.

For years, she had lived with the worry of being judged for something that was completely out of her control and is surprisingly frequent in this country. Working in the exclusive atmosphere of the White House, she had assumed that having an incarcerated parent made her a "only." But this was most likely not the case. According to government figures, more than five million children in the United States have had a parent in jail or prison at some point in their lives—roughly 7% of all youngsters. It goes to the reason that Chynna was probably not as isolated as she believed. Nobody, of course, was talking about it. Why should they? We often believe—and rightly so, given the culture of judgement we live in—that keeping our vulnerabilities hidden keeps us safe.

What this means is that many of us are led to believe that we are "only" when we are not. Our vaults can alienate us from others, deepening the agony of invisibility. That's a difficult path to take. The amount we keep hidden away and guarded by instinctual feelings of fear or shame might add to a greater sensation that we don't belong or matter—that our truth can never comfortably mesh with the reality of the world we live in. We never know who else is out there, who else might understand or even be helped by whatever it is we're holding back by keeping our weaknesses hidden.

A year or two after our original talk, Chynna appeared as a guest on a Spotify podcast series I was presenting, joining a discussion about mentor-mentee relationships. During the conversation, she discussed growing up with a father in prison, saying she'd learned to let go of the shame she'd always associated with this part of her story and had come to see how it helped shape her into the successful person she is today.

Chynna accomplished something not only for herself but also for others by making her tale more visible. Messages began to pour in from all around the country almost immediately after the show aired, a bright and lovely chorus of people wanting to respond to her. They thanked her for her words. Many people—older, younger, and even some children—wrote in to say they knew exactly how she felt, having had to negotiate the strains of having a loved one in prison and figuring out how to share the narrative, how to fit it into their own journey.

The fact that Chynna spoke with composure and pleasure in herself rather than embarrassment was very telling. That was also a part of her story. It raised them all in various ways, providing a larger sphere in which they could feel seen and know they belonged. The fact that a small girl who'd seen the inside of the federal penitentiary's family visit room had also seen the inside of the White House meant something to them.

When someone chooses to unveil the source code for her steadfastness and power by lifting the curtain on a perceived flaw in her story, on a circumstance or condition that may usually be deemed a weakness. And, as we've seen many times throughout history, the strength of one determined person can become the strength of many. I reflected on this when, on January 20, 2021, a young writer named Amanda Gorman stepped up to the microphone in a sunny yellow coat and electrified an audience of millions by reciting a poem perfectly tuned to one of the most fraught and complicated moments in recent history.

Just two weeks previously, a crowd of around 2,000 individuals had overrun the United States Capitol, attempting to prevent Congress from certifying Joe Biden's electoral victory. They'd smashed windows, hammered down doors, attacked and injured police officers, and broken into the Senate chambers, scaring our leaders and jeopardising democracy itself. Barack and I had been watching the news in disbelief as it happened live. The events of that day shook me to my core. I knew our country was in the grip of a toxic level of political division, but witnessing the rhetoric escalate into reckless, rage-filled violence intended at reversing an election was sad. Seeing an American president promote a siege on his own government was one of the most terrifying things I'd ever seen.

We had not always agreed with our elected officials as citizens. But, as Americans, we had historically placed our faith in the larger enterprise of democracy, a set of values in which we had placed our trust. As First Lady, I'd met dozens of hardworking and thoughtful government employees, people who'd dedicated their lives to public service, with many of them offering knowledge and continuity across numerous presidential administrations, regardless of which party was in power. I'd seen the same thing in state government in Illinois, where Barack was a legislator, and in city government in Chicago, where I worked for the mayor's administration. Leaders came and went, they were voted in and out, but the government itself—a peaceful, participatory democracy based on the concept of free elections—always remained and always functioned, like a slow-rotating wheel. None of it was ideal, but it was our union's, our United States', contract. It is what created and sustains our freedom.

Though order was eventually restored, and congressional leaders were able to certify the election that same night, the damage done on January 6 was immense; it felt as if the nation's mind had been ripped apart. The trauma was real, and the pain was palpable. As Inauguration Day approached, tensions were high. The FBI issued a statement warning of additional potential violence, putting all fifty states on high alert. To be honest, I was worried about what might happen.

It was evident, however, that a choice had to be made between fear and faith, not just for those of us who would sit on the inauguration stage to witness the swearing-in of a newly elected president, but for the nation as a whole. What position would we take? Would we show up for our own democracy even if there was uncertainty in the air? Could we maintain our composure and resolve? I'd done the same thing four years before for a president whose candidacy I hadn't supported and whose leadership I didn't trust. I wasn't happy about it, but I showed up anyway. I was there to support and elevate the bigger process, as well as to assist enforce a higher creed. Inaugurations were simply a ritual recommitment to the pursuit of our values, a call to adapt to whatever reality our larger electorate had brought, and to keep going.

The stakes felt bigger than ever this time. Could we tune out the background noise and rediscover our faith?

I'd chosen a comfortable and practical wardrobe for the inauguration with the advice of my longtime stylist Meredith Koop, a plum-coloured wool coat over a matching turtleneck and leggings and brought together with an oversized gold belt. I chose a pair of block-heeled boots and black gloves. I didn't have a purse and wore a face mask (of course). Barack and I had gotten many security briefings in advance of the event, and we left for the Capitol that day feeling pretty comfortable. I told Chynna, who would normally have attended me and waited in a backstage holding room during the ceremony, to stay at home as a precaution.

I took Barack's hand and proceeded onto the inaugural platform, attempting to embody the audacity that seemed to be required. As we took our seats, I did what I'd done at three previous inaugurations: I took a deep breath and focused my calm.

You could feel everything in the air that morning on the National Mall—the tension and determination, the profound longing for change, the anxiety brought on by the pandemic, the spectre of the violence we'd witnessed at the Capitol, the broader concerns about where we were headed, and the sunshine of a new day. Everything was there, lingering and unspoken, contradicting and unnerving. We'd convened once more for the sake of history. We'd been given another chance to tell the American tale, to let the wheel turn, thanks to the democratic process. But no one had yet spoken it into being.

Until one woman came up and read her poem to us.

Amanda Gorman's delivery that day was bubbly. Her voice was a force to be reckoned with. She possesses uncommon oratory talents for anyone, let alone a twenty-two-year-old, and she used her remarks that day to restore hope to a drooping, grieving nation. Don't give up, the verse said. Continue your efforts.

Here's an excerpt from the poem's final rallying call. It's worth reading aloud, like with any other work of poetry:

So let us leave a better country than the one we were given.

We will transform this wounded world into a wondrous one with every breath from our bronze-pounded chests.

We will rise from the West's gold-limned heights!

We shall rise from the windswept Northeast, where our predecessors first recognized the possibility of revolution!

We will rise from the Midwestern cities with lakefronts!

We will rise from the sweltering South!

We'll rebuild, reconcile, and heal...

Her poem recalled our country's story at a time when we needed to remember our fortitude. She was able to calm a lot of people down with that. I believe she managed to change the attitude and almost miraculously dispel a lot of dread that day, encouraging not only hope but courage. What I didn't realise at the time was that Amanda Gorman had grown up with an auditory-processing issue and, as a result, had spent most of her life battling a speech impediment—one that caused her to have specific difficulty pronouncing the sound of the letter r. She couldn't even say her own last name correctly until she was nearly twenty years old. You might wish to go back and reread the sentence above, making sure to remember every r. See how that affects your astonishment.

When I interviewed Gorman not long after the inauguration, she stated that she'd learned to see her speech impairment as less of a hindrance and more of a blessing. To be sure, the difficulties she'd had when learning to pronounce words had been painful, but they'd also propelled her further into a practice of investigating and experimenting with sound and language, first as a child, then as a teen, and now as a lionhearted young poet. The effort required to overcome the limitation had led her to uncover new abilities in herself.

"For a long time, I saw it as a weakness," she admitted. "Now I really look at it as a strength." She'd turned what felt like a flaw into a valuable asset, something potent and effective. The ailment she'd had her entire life—what distinguished her from other students at school, what most would consider a disadvantage—had also enabled her to become who she was.

We'd witnessed a young woman achieving a zenith in her powerful performance on the initial stage. But that was just one day in her life, one chapter in her journey, and she wanted to make sure others understood what she'd gone through. Gorman has made an effort to underline that her achievement was not quick and that she relied on others for support along the way—family members, speech therapists, teachers—now that she is in the public eye and being praised as a dazzling talent. "I want to emphasise that this took a lifetime and a village," she said. Her most conspicuous triumph came only after years of tiny setbacks and gradual growth. She advanced one step for every r she managed to master. With each new step, she became more aware of her own strength and agency. She had proclaimed her way into confidence, and in the midst of doing so, she had discovered the source code for her strength. She knew how to own it now that she knew what it was. It was hers to retain and use for the rest of her life. And there were plenty of other peaks she wanted to scale.

"Especially for girls of colour, we're treated as if we're lightning or gold in the pan—we're not treated as things that are going to last," she remarked. "You must truly believe that what I'm about and what I'm here for extends far beyond this moment." I'm discovering that I'm not lighting that strikes only once. I am the hurricane that comes every year, and you will see me again soon." Many successful people I know have learnt to channel their adversity in this manner. They serve as a training ground for them. This does not suggest that the most successful among us have overcome all obstacles or are strolling about seeing rainbows and unicorns where others see oppressive systems or walls that are simply too high to scale. It usually just means that they've done exactly what Gorman's poem challenged us all to do: don't give up. Continue your efforts.

I see brilliant and creative people making their way up the ladder of power and prominence all around me, many of whom have worked out how to harness rather than hide what makes them unique. When we do this, we begin to recognize all of the paradoxes and influences that make us who we are. We normalise diversity. More of the wider human mosaic is revealed. We make everyone's tale a little better.

Ali Wong, a caustic, truth-spitting comedian, is one of my favourite comedians to watch. She originally piqued my interest in 2016 when she released a stand-up special called Baby Cobra on Netflix. She takes the stage at seven and a half months pregnant, wearing a short, body-hugging dress and red horn-rimmed spectacles, looking amazing and almost defiantly female while delivering a bawdy, no-holds-barred monologue about sex, race, fertility, and parenthood. She is fierce, sensual, and real all at the same time, led by, constrained by, and completely unaffected by the orb of her belly. She reveals herself to an enthralling effect.

A reporter for The New Yorker once asked Wong what she tells younger comics who want to know the secret to making it in the world of comedy, where she is still in the minority as an Asian American woman with small children. Wong responded that the key for her was to not see any of those things as barriers. "You simply shift your perspective and say to yourself, 'Wait a minute: I'm a woman!'" "And the majority of stand-up comedians are men," she added. "You know what masculine comics aren't capable of? They are unable to conceive. They are unable to perform while pregnant. So, in my opinion, just use all of those differences."

Our differences are both treasures and tools. They are valuable, valid, worthy, and necessary to communicate. Recognizing this in ourselves and others, we begin to rewrite more and more stories about not-mattering. We begin to shift paradigms about who belongs, making more room for more people. We can decrease the loneliness of not belonging by taking small steps.

The goal is to adjust our attitudes and appreciate the importance of difference in ourselves and others, seeing it as a reason to take a stride forward rather than a step back, to stand rather than sit, to speak more rather than less. The work is difficult. It frequently necessitates audacity. And there are no promises as to how it will be received. But every time someone succeeds, every time another tightrope is crossed, we see more perspectives shift. When a pregnant Asian American comedian makes millions of people laugh, it matters. When a twenty-two-year-old Black woman steps up and nearly single-handedly resets the atmosphere of a nation, it matters. It matters when a Muslim becomes CEO or a transgender person wins class president. It matters when we feel secure enough to be ourselves without fear of being judged, and when we can speak frankly about the experiences that shaped us into the persons we are. And, as we've seen in recent years, it matters when we can confirm a strong voice and lessen another person's isolation with words as simple as "me too."

All of these stories broaden our understanding of what is possible. They also help us to better grasp the various aspects of being human. There's suddenly more to see as a result of them. The world we live in begins to appear larger and more complicated, a more accurate portrayal of the vast and nuanced place that it is. Never give up. Continue your efforts. It's a worthy motto, but I can't go on without addressing the unfairness buried within it. The labour of visibility is difficult and poorly dispersed. In reality, nothing about it is fair. I am all too familiar with the burdens of representation and the false standards for perfection that exacerbate the hills that so many of us are attempting to climb. We continue to ask much too much of those who are marginalised and far too little of those who are not.

Please keep this in mind as I advise you to consider your challenges as building bricks and your weaknesses as strengths. None of this is said carelessly. Nothing seems straightforward to me. My own experience has taught me that the risks are real, and the work is never done. Not only that, but many of us are already exhausted, cautious, fearful, or depressed for legitimate reasons. As previously said, the barriers you meet are frequently pre-planned; they are land mines buried within systems and structures whose authority is based on the belonging of certain but not all people. It can feel overwhelming to try to overcome, especially if you believe you are working alone. I'd like to remind you once more of the power of simple actions, small gestures, and small ways you can allow yourself to reset and replenish. Nobody can be a lion or a hurricane. But it doesn't imply your efforts will go unnoticed. Or that your tale should be kept private.

The simple truth is that there will be disappointments for many of us. You can work your butt off to get to a position of prominence and relative influence in this world and still have your heart fall when you are there. You can hike all the way up to whatever summit you want to reach—a career, a school, an opportunity—carrying the dreams and expectations of your loved ones with you, batting away messages of shame and otherness like a superhero as you go. And when the climb finally ends and you arrive, exhausted and sweating, at that high point with the beautiful view you've long desired, there's one thing you're almost always guaranteed to see: an air-conditioned luxury tour bus and a group of people who did none of the work, having been driven straight up an access road, their picnic blankets already laid out, their party well underway.

It's a depressing sensation. I've seen it and seen it firsthand. There will be times—perhaps many times—when you will need to take a deep breath and re-establish your balance. You may look around and have to tell yourself that you are stronger and thinner as a result of the journey, of carrying the weight on your back. You can persuade yourself that having to negotiate uneven terrain has made you nimble, and you may feel better for it.

That doesn't make it any less unfair. When you complete the job, though, you own the talents. They cannot be taken or lost. They are yours to keep and use indefinitely. That is what I hope you remember the most. There is one more irony to mention: People may accuse you of taking shortcuts or being unworthy of your location on the hill for whatever work you put in and wherever you end up. They'll have a slew of terms at their disposal—affirmative action, scholarship kid, gender quota, or diversity hire—and they'll wield them with contempt. The message is well-known: I don't believe you are entitled to what you have.

All I can say is don't bother listening. Don't let that poison get inside of you. Consider the following story: NBC executives chose to adapt a hit British sitcom for American television almost twenty years ago. To begin work on the scripts, the network hired a group of eight writers. There were only two people of colour in the group, one of whom happened to be the lone lady as well. She was twenty-four at the time. It was her first time writing for television, and she was terrified. She was not only a double minority, but she was also dealing with an extra layer of self-consciousness, having been hired under NBC's relatively new diversity drive. She was concerned that, as a diversity recruit, she would be perceived as less of a talent and more as someone whose existence was only to check a box.

"For a long time, I was really embarrassed about it," the author subsequently admitted to an interviewer. "No one mentioned it to me, but they were all aware. And I was well aware of it." She compared the sensation to wearing a scarlet letter, which kept her on the outside.

Mindy Kaling was her name. The show in question was The Office. She ended up being one of its stars for eight seasons. She also authored twenty-two of the show's episodes, more than any other writer, and became the first woman of colour to be nominated for an Emmy for comedy writing.

Kaling now speaks frequently and proudly about being a diversity hire, claiming that it is an important part of her story and that it is vital for others to understand what it took for her to get to where she is professionally. It's not something to store away. She was able to let go of her self-consciousness and doubts once she began to better understand the advantages her colleagues had arrived with in the first place, the connections that came from the familiarity and privilege of being white and male within a system built and maintained largely by others like them. "It took me a while to realise that I was just getting the access that other people had because of who they knew," she adds.

She could have taken a step back, but instead she took a stride forward. She survived the discomfort of being "only," focused on the task, and as a result, she was able to make more room for others coming up behind her, allowing for more storytellers and stories. She literally wrote her way to fame. Of course, Kaling has since become a force in her business, developing, producing, writing, and starring in a slew of blockbuster television shows and films, nearly all of which feature the tales of women of colour. She has broadened the horizon of belonging through her art.

When we tell our stories fully and honestly, we frequently discover that we're less alone and more linked than we ever imagined. We collaborate to build new platforms. I've felt this in profound ways at various moments in my life, the most humbling being in the months after the publication of Becoming. I was astounded by the number of people who attended my gatherings, ready to bond over what we shared. They came bearing their tales. They displayed their emotions. They had experienced what it was like to have a parent with MS. They'd had miscarriages and lost friends to cancer. They knew what it was like to fall in love with someone who throws your life off course.

"Language is a finding place, not a hiding place," writer Jeanette Winterson observed, and I have found this to be true. I discovered more community than I'd ever known by opening my vault and shedding some light on the times when I'd felt most vulnerable or out of control. Yes, I was already "well-known" at the time, but this was something new. The broad strokes of my story had been told many times—by me and others—but now that I had the time and energy to write a book and was free of the political world my husband inhabited for the first time in decades, I found myself filling in the blanks with feelings and experiences that were more personal, less likely to appear on a Wikipedia page or in a magazine profile. I showed myself from the inside out with the book, less guarded than I'd ever been, and I was amazed at how readily people dropped their guards in reaction.

Almost none of the topics readers were eager to discuss with me had anything to do with our skin colour or political party affiliation. Our common ground appeared to reach past those things, almost dwarfing them, and it wasn't exactly exalted or glamorous territory either. Nobody approached me at book events, eager to tell me about the time they wore a ball gown, spoke with a congressman, or took a White House tour. Nobody cared about my professional life or accomplishments. Instead, we talked about how many of us had insisted on a nearly all-peanut-butter diet as kids, or struggled to find the right career as adults, or needed two tries to pass a licensing exam, or had a dog that couldn't be house-trained, or a spouse who was always late. It was the mundane grind of being human, I discovered, that established the bridges between us, prioritising what made us alike over what made us different. I can't even begin to describe how frequently women approached me in cities across the country, gripping my hands tightly, looking into my eyes, and saying, "You know when you talk about eating a Chipotle bowl in your car at the strip mall during your lunch break and that counts as your 'me-time'? That's exactly how I felt. That is also my life."

I felt the possibilities for a kind of understanding that went beyond the things we shared with each small point of connection between us. Because, for everything that we have in common, there is plenty that we do not. We are unique. I can't genuinely know the innermost contours of my life or sentiments any more than you can. I'll never truly grasp what it's like to be from Tucson, Vietnam, or Syria. I can't imagine what it's like to be awaiting a military deployment, farming sorghum in Iowa, flying an aeroplane, or struggling with addiction. I have my own Black and female experiences, but it doesn't mean I can understand what anyone else's Black and female body has gone through.

All I can do is strive to get closer to your uniqueness, to feel connected by our minor overlaps. This is how empathy functions. It's how difference becomes woven into togetherness. Empathy bridges the gaps between us, but it never completely fills them. We are drawn into the lives of others by what they feel comfortable and capable of showing us, as well as the generosity with which we are able to meet them. We begin to comprehend the world more fully, piece by piece, person by person.

I believe the most we can ever accomplish is walk halfway across the bridge toward another person and be grateful for the opportunity to be there at all. I used to think about it when I laid in bed with Sasha and Malia at night. I'd watch them fall asleep, their lips parted, the arcs of their little chests rising and falling beneath the sheets, and be struck by the awareness that no matter how hard I tried, I'd never know even half of what they were thinking. We're all alone, each of us. That's what it's like to be human.

What we owe each other is the opportunity to construct whatever platforms we can between us, even if they're built of peanut butter and Chipotle bowls and only get us halfway. This is not an argument for openly disclosing all of your secrets. It doesn't mean you have to do something huge and visible, like write a book or appear on a podcast. There is no obligation to reveal every inner agony or every thought in your thoughts. Maybe you just listen for a bit. Perhaps you can become a safe vessel for other people's tales, practising what it's like to receive another person's truth with respect and remembering to safeguard the dignity of those who are brave enough to share openly. Be trustworthy and sensitive to your acquaintances' stories. Maintain confidentiality and avoid gossip. Read works by people whose perspectives differ from yours, listen to voices you haven't heard before, and seek out new narratives. You might end up finding more places for yourself in and with them.

There is no way to eradicate the agony of being human, but I believe we can lessen it. This begins when we challenge ourselves to become less frightened to share and more willing to listen—when the entirety of your story adds to the entirety of mine. I saw some of you. You get a glimpse of me. We can't know everything, but as familiars, we're better off. When we hold hands with another person and recognize some part of their narrative, we are accepting and affirming two truths at the same time: we are lonely, yet we are not alone.

CHAPTER 8

THE ARMOUR WE WEAR

When I deliver a significant speech, I strive to memorise all of the words long before I take the stage. I practise and prepare for weeks ahead of time, leaving as little to chance as possible. The first time I appeared live on television in front of a large national audience was in 2008, when I delivered a prime-time address at Denver's Pepsi Center during the Democratic National Convention. This was just a few months before the election, when Barack and I were still presenting ourselves to the public, and it was a little disaster.

Craig, my brother, had been picked as my warm-up act that evening. He offered a wonderful introduction, concluding by inviting everyone to join him in welcoming "my little sister and our nation's next First Lady, Michelle Obama!" to the stage. As I went out from the wings, the audience erupted in cheers. I met Craig halfway to the podium and hugged him, my nerves jangling but knowing that my brother was there to steady me with a final supportive word. Craig drew me in closer as he wrapped his arms around me, pressing his lips to my ear so I could hear him over the upbeat music and roaring throng of over 20,000 people. I expected him to congratulate me with a "You got this!" or "I'm proud of you, sis!" but instead he bent down and muttered, "Left prompter is OUT."

Before we parted ways, Craig and I offered each other exaggerated it's-all-good, we're-on-live-television smiles. Meanwhile, my mind was racing as I tried to digest his statements. I made my way to the rostrum, waving at the audience, feeling as if I wasn't even in my own body, all the while wondering, What did he just say?

I took my spot in front of the microphone and sought to compose myself, taking advantage of the extended applause to get my bearings. I cast a quick glance to the left, solving the enigma in real time. One of the two teleprompters had died due to a technical problem. This meant that whenever I looked to the left side of the arena, I wouldn't be able to see the text of my address projected on the glass screen of a teleprompter, which had been placed precisely to assist me maintain my cadence and stay on cue. The screen was completely blank. I was standing there on live television, knowing I had to speak for the next sixteen minutes. There was no stopping the show or requesting assistance. For a split second, I felt completely alone—and also completely exposed.

I kept grinning. I continued to wave. I kept buying time, attempting to calm my anxiety. The audience was now on its feet, whooping and cheering. I swiftly looked in the opposite direction to ensure that the right-side teleprompter was still operational. That's all right, I thought. I also remembered that I had another tool to rely on, something called the "confidence monitor," which was a massive digital screen set up in the centre of the arena, slightly above the crowd and just below the bank of network news cameras that were filming everything. The confidence monitor, like the teleprompter, would scroll the contents of my speech in enormous letters, allowing me to look directly into the cameras while keeping track of my lines. We'd done a practice run earlier in the day in the vast, empty stadium, and everything had gone flawlessly. When I realised it was time to speak, I looked around for encouragement from the presence of the confidence monitor in the middle of the venue. That's when I understood we had a new problem.

The Democratic Party had created and distributed thousands of gorgeous blue-and-white Michelle placards in advance of my appearance. Every third person in the crowd seemed to be energetically waving one aloft. The placards had been designed vertically rather than horizontally, maybe to keep anyone from getting smacked inside all the waving. Each one was several feet tall and slim, a narrow slat-like rectangle with a long handle attached. Nobody seemed to have foreseen, however, that after people got out of their chairs and held their signs up to show their support, all those slats formed a massive, swaying barrier, one so tall and dense that it almost completely obscured the words displayed on my confidence monitor. I couldn't see much of anything.

One of the most important lessons I've learned in my life is that adaptation and preparedness are inextricably intertwined. Preparedness is an element of the armour I wear. Before anything that resembles a test, I plan, rehearse, and complete my homework. This allows me to operate more calmly in stressful situations, knowing that no matter what occurs, I will eventually find a way out. Being organised and prepared allows me to feel more secure on the court.

Craig used to put our family through rigorous and regularly scheduled fire drills, making sure that the four of us knew every possible exit from our small apartment, that we'd practised opening various windows, finding the fire extinguishers, and that, if necessary, we could carry our father's weakened body down the stairs. It all seemed a little dramatic at the time, but I now realise why it was important. Craig, as previously said, was a natural worrier, and this was his way of channelling his anxieties into something more concrete and actionable. He was making our family more nimble by teaching us every possible escape route and how to survive something difficult. He wanted us to be aware of all our alternatives and to have rehearsed using every tool at our disposal so that we would have a broad range of options if calamity came. This is a lesson that I will never forget. Preparedness serves as a buffer against panic. And it is terror that will lead you to ruin.

That night in Denver, I relied on the one thing I knew I could bank on—something I'd rely on many times over the next eight years—my own readiness. I had managed to arm myself against panic after weeks of diligent and slightly apprehensive preparation. Every syllable of that speech was learned and practised by me. I knew it from the inside out. I'd spent countless hours writing it, practising it, and running through the phrases until one line flowed easily into the next, until every rhythm felt natural and easy—a true depiction of my emotions. In that vulnerable and exposed moment, I had one last line of defence: I'd practised the fire drill. I could stop worrying about everything that was broken or blocked and instead rely on what was in my intellect and heart. Even with my nerves frayed and tens of thousands of people watching, even with a faulty teleprompter and a confidence monitor obscured by a sea of waving placards, I had everything I needed. I chatted for the next sixteen minutes without pausing.

I've always appreciated the sensation of accomplishment, of overcoming obstacles and talking myself out of dread. I wanted to live a large life, even though I had no concept what it meant or how a youngster from Chicago's South Side went about attaining one. I just knew I wanted to shoot for the stars. I wanted to be the best.

Like many children, I was captivated by stories of pioneers, explorers, hurdle jumpers, and envelope pushers—anyone who pushed the boundaries of what appeared imaginable. I borrowed books from the library about Amelia Earhart, Wilma Rudolph, and Rosa Parks. Pippi Longstocking, the fabled red-headed Swedish girl who crossed the seven seas with her pet monkey and a suitcase full of wealth, was a hero of mine.

Some of those journeys stayed with me when I fell asleep at night. I aspired to be a boundary pusher and a margin mover, but I was not naive. I was aware of the counter narrative that existed for kids like me even when I was little. Already, I could feel the pressure of low expectations, a pervasive sense that as a Black girl from a working-class neighbourhood, I wasn't supposed to amount to much or go very far.

This feeling pervaded not only my school, but also my city and the rest of my country. It's strange but true—and, I believe, quite common—to know as a child that you are smart and capable of all kinds of perfection, but to also sense that much of the world has a completely different opinion of you. It's a difficult place to begin. It can develop a sense of desperation and necessitates attention. My school was dividing pupils into "learning tracks" as early as first grade, selecting a small group of overachievers for higher-level instruction while leaving the other students behind, investing less in them, and assigning them to a lower place within the wider system. We may have been too little to describe what was going on around us, but I believe many of us were aware of it. You were aware that if you made one mistake, stumbled, or had a distracting family crisis, you may be promptly and often permanently demoted to the group that received less.

When you're a child in this kind of setting, you can feel it in your bones that your options are limited and fleeting. Success is a lifeboat that must be pursued. Striking for perfection is an attempt to keep from drowning.

The good news is that ambition can be tantalisingly pure when you're young, a pulsating certainty that, despite everything, you're unstoppable, that you've got what it takes. This blend of dream and drive is something that burns brightly within you. It's what Tiffany, the aforementioned youngster, meant when she said, "I want to take over like Beyoncé, but bigger."

However, whether it's breaking into a certain professional sector, performing on a major stage, or achieving substantial social change, life will undoubtedly complicate any desire at some time. The boundaries are rapidly revealed. Obstacles appear. There are sceptics. Injustice clogs the road. Practical concerns will frequently emerge. Money becomes scarce. As time passes, the trade-offs become more numerous, and they are frequently unavoidable. Ask anyone who has gotten even halfway to where they want to go. Getting where you want to go will nearly always feel like a battle at some time.

This is when agility comes into play. You must begin to play both offence and defence simultaneously, pushing yourself forward but also doubling back to guard your resources, advancing toward your goals without completely exhausting your strength. It can rapidly become difficult. You will also need to arm yourself. If you want to tear down barriers and knock down walls, I've discovered that you must first locate and preserve your own boundaries, keeping track of your time, energy, health, and spirit as you go. The universe turns out to be full with lines and limitations, some of which are difficult to cross, some of which are necessary to cross, and others of which should be exploded entirely. Many of us spend our entire lives trying to figure out which lines we cross and which we don't.

The point is that nobody survives a hero's journey undefended. The challenge in leading a big life becomes trying to find ways to protect your dreams and your drive, to remain tough without being overly guarded, to stay nimble and open to growth, allowing others to see you for who you are. It's about learning how to shelter your flame without hiding its light.

I met Tyne, a bright and vivacious young woman, a few years ago. She worked in book publishing and had come to our offices in Washington with a number of her colleagues to discuss my ideas for this new book.

Tyne mentioned something that had particularly remained with her after reading Becoming during that chat. It was a brief anecdote in which I described how, during my first visit to England as First Lady, while attending a reception at Buckingham Palace and feeling a moment of warm connection inside of a conversation, I instinctively reached out and placed a loving hand on the Queen of England's shoulder. Her Majesty, who was eighty-two years old at the time, looked unconcerned. In fact, she'd answered by sliding her arm over my back. Nonetheless, our exchange had been captured on camera, sending shockwaves through the British press and generating headlines across the world. "Michelle Obama Dares to Hug the Queen!" I was accused of being disrespectful, of defying royal conventions, of upsetting the established order. The implication was not subtle: I was a trespasser, undeserving of the company I kept.

I had no clue you couldn't touch the Queen of England. In that unusual first year as First Lady, and in that strange royal environment, all I'd tried to do was be myself.

This story took up only a few pages of my memoir, but it had remained with Tyne. Why? Because she was able to read between the lines. As a woman of colour, she recognized a sentiment that we both shared: the continual problem of feeling comfortable in areas when you are a minority.

For her, working in book publishing—a field typically driven by white people and shaped by their concerns—was symbolically equivalent to being invited to a reception at Buckingham Palace. We were both aware of the discomfort. There were lineups everywhere. These places were dense with subtle protocols and old traditions, leaving newcomers with a steep, if not impossible, learning curve to navigate and no guidebook to guide them. There were enough subtle signs to tell us that we barely belonged, that our presence was virtually experimental, reliant on us adhering to someone else's idea of good behaviour. Nobody needed to say anything because the past was so deep: for a long time, persons like us would have been stopped at the gates.

Even when you make it inside, you don't readily shed your sensation of being an outsider, as I've discovered. There's a tension that clings to you like a cloud. You can't help but wonder: When will this get easier?

Many of us "code-switch" to get by, altering our behaviour, look, or way of speech to better fit into the culture of our company. As many kids do, I realised the importance of code-switching early in life and used it as a tool to get around. My parents instilled in us the value of what they considered "proper" language, encouraging us, for example, to say "aren't" rather than "ain't." When I carried that diction out into my neighbourhood, other kids would swiftly mock me, accusing me of being "uppity" or "talking like a white girl." Not wanting to be left out, I'd make some changes, presenting myself more like those kids. Later, when I arrived at schools like Princeton and Harvard, I relied heavily on my ostensibly uppity diction to get by, presenting myself more like the people around me in the hopes of avoiding stereotypes.

Over time, I became increasingly good at reading the surroundings I was in, picking up on subtle indications from those around me. During my time working for the City of Chicago, I learned almost unconsciously how to adjust my behaviour to fit the existing vibe and context, whether it was a South Side community meeting attended by mostly blue-collar African American women, a corporate board meeting full of wealthy white men, or eventually an audience with the Queen of England. I grew more adaptable and fluid in my communication, and I felt it let me connect with more people, extending myself over lines of race, gender, and class. I didn't overthink it since I felt like I had no choice but to make those changes throughout most of my life.

In this regard, code-switching has historically been a survival strategy for many BIPOC. As much as it is typically a reaction to negative stereotypes, it can also function as a kind of passport: I utilised it to get myself further, across more barriers, and into areas where I would not have fit at all otherwise.

However, there are drawbacks to standardising this type of activity or perceiving it as a long-term path to fairness. Many people react not only to the stress of constantly making adjustments, but also to the fundamental unfairness of the premise, especially when those adjustments involve concealing or minimising one's racial, ethnic, or gender identity in order to advance professionally or make those who aren't marginalised feel more at ease. What are we giving up? Who does it benefit? To be accepted, are we compromising too much or suppressing our true selves? This raises a fundamental and broad point concerning inclusivity: why should individuals try to alter themselves when it is their workplace that has to change?

The difficulty is that these are difficult questions and significant societal concerns to grapple with, especially when most of us are just trying to get through the day. Code-switching can be exhausting, but so can confronting systemic bias, even with something as seemingly basic as dressing comfortably or wearing your natural hairstyle to work. Either way, the options can be pricey. Tyne said that even years into her career and after multiple promotions, she still struggled with feeling like a foreigner at work, attempting to understand a culture that didn't always seem like hers. She was always monitoring the boundaries, she claimed, understanding that her acceptance depended on her capacity to adapt to the conventions of others—to seem as less "other" herself. She explained that she had been purposefully limiting her code-switching at work in order to alleviate some of her self-consciousness about being a Black woman in a white workplace. She believed that spending less time thinking about breaking some unsaid norm and more time trying to feel more like herself would assist her professionally. But she was assessing the dangers, knowing that for someone like her, a casual approach could be interpreted as an overreach."Pretty much every day at work," she said, "I feel like I'm deciding whether or not to hug the Queen."

I've been thinking a lot about Tyne's comment since then, struck by the metaphor's potency. What she articulated rang true for me; it was a sensation I'd struggled with for much of my professional life. It was akin to the stress that many of my acquaintances described feeling at work, the difficulties that come with navigating a set of invisible lines and determining the difference between reach and overreach.

They, like Tyne, found themselves evaluating the dangers and rewards of removing some of their armour in order to be seen and heard as themselves. Whose set of rules am I following? How careful should I be? How confident are you? How genuine? In many cases, individuals were attempting to figure out whether they could stay in their jobs—whether they'd have enough bandwidth to develop and prosper, or whether too much hiding or worrying would eventually lead to feelings of demoralisation and burnout.

Years ago, when I first started my career in corporate law, I got to know a few of the women who worked above me in the office, those who had made partners at the huge international company where we worked, frequently against great odds. They'd spent years ascending the hierarchical ladder, traversing a power system that had been constructed, managed, and preserved almost entirely by men, extending all the way back to the firm's inception by two Civil War veterans in 1866. These women were always welcoming and supportive of me, and they were truly interested in my achievement. I couldn't help but notice that they carried themselves with the gruff bearing of pioneers.

Most of them were tough as nails, pushed for time, and running a very tight ship at work. It was unusual to hear any of them speak about their relatives. Nobody ever raced off to a Little League game or a paediatrician's visit, as far as I can recall. The boundaries were completely intact. Their armour was on, and their personal lives were almost miraculously hidden away. There was little room for the warm and fuzzy. Their perfection had almost an edge to it. When I first started, I noticed that a number of my female superiors seemed to be looking at me with suspicion, as if they were asking, essentially, "Can she grind?" They were secretly examining if my legal abilities and level of devotion would match theirs, whether I would be able to keep up and so not jeopardise the status of women in general within the firm. This, of course, was another bad feature of being among the "onlies" in a fortress that was not meant for us. We were all grouped together, which added to the stress on everyone. Our fortunes seemed to be intertwined. If you mess up, we all mess up. Everyone understood what was at stake. What these female partners were communicating—what they had to signal, really—was that their standards were significantly higher than everyone else's at the firm. They'd earned their way beyond the gates and into the club, but it felt as if their admission was always conditional, as if they'd never stop having to prove they belonged.

As a young female lawyer, I recall reading in The New York Times about a survey that revealed how tired and frustrated lawyers, particularly women, were with their professions. It brought up a slew of troubling issues for me as I considered everything I'd put into my still-young profession, all the school loans I'd taken out, all the hours I'd already put in. I had to decide what kind of future I wanted for myself, how much agony I was willing to tolerate or endure. What duty did I have to model excellence and strive for overachievement only to justify occupying a position that might otherwise be filled by a man? What authority did I have to alter a culture based on these norms? And how much energy could I conjure for that specific fight in that specific sphere?

The women who had blazed a trail inside the world of corporate law were, for the most part, living lives I didn't envy, making sacrifices I wasn't sure I was ready or able to make myself. But the fact that I got to see any of it, that I got to be there at all, and that I had some freedom to choose how I wanted to live my life was mainly owing to the effort they'd put in, the armour they'd put on. These women had borne the brunt of breaking down previously closed doors, allowing a new generation to more easily analyse, fight for change, or retreat as we saw fit. They'd constructed the platform I'm now standing on.

It's easy to judge one's forefathers and their choices, to judge them for their concessions or to hold them accountable for changes they couldn't make. To younger people, the quantity of armour worn by an older generation may appear inflexible and archaic, but it is crucial to recognize the context. The fact that more and more Black women feel free to bring their full aesthetic into their professional lives, to wear their hair braided or in dreads to work, or that young people can sport body modifications or dyed hair without feeling othered, or that women have protected breastfeeding spaces at work, has a lot to do with the work done by people like those female partners at my law firm. They had to prove themselves in order for the rest of us to have to prove ourselves a little less.

I eventually drew a line that worked for me. I took a risk by leaving law practice and went on to specifically seek out positions with a different kind of governing code, jobs that would allow me to at least periodically sneak out for dance recitals and paediatrician's appointments. I quit the legal profession because I knew I'd be more passionate and productive working somewhere else. But the mentorship I gained at that law firm, particularly from the senior women, provided me with something I needed to carry into the White House. They taught me how to carefully consider how I wanted to pick my battles and manage my own resources. They taught me that in order to even start changing a paradigm, you must have a thick skin and double down on professional discipline and hard effort. None of it was perfect, but it was the reality of the situation at the time. It was also, in some ways, a continuation of my education about life on the frontier, confirmation of what I'd learned at Princeton and, later, Harvard Law School—not through the book-learning parts, but through the experience of being a double minority, of being an outsider in the most insider places. You needed to be both armoured and agile. You had to be tough to get through it.

I believe that nearly everyone wears some form of armour to work. And quite rightly so. In some senses, it's one of the professional tenets: You've been tasked with bringing a harder, stronger version of yourself to work. You keep your flaws in check and your messes mostly at home. You set boundaries and expect your coworkers and supervisors to do the same. After all, you're there to accomplish a job, not to become lifelong friends or to work out your personal difficulties or the personal troubles of others. Whether you're teaching middle schoolers, running a health clinic, baking pizza, or leading a software firm, you're supposed to contribute to the bigger enterprise, to exercise discipline, and to keep your sentiments stored for the most part. Work becomes your primary focus and commitment. It is the reason you are compensated.

And yet, no human endeavour is ever this neat. There are no clear lines left. In some ways, the epidemic was beneficial, while in others it was detrimental, because it exposed more discrepancies and truths between us. As we've attempted videoconferences with toddlers squirming on our laps against the backdrop of our half-cleaned kitchens, and as many of us continue to try to conduct business despite yapping dogs and roommates on nearby screens, we've seen the boundaries blur and the clutter increase, possibly underscoring what's always been true: We are complete and uncontainable people living complete and uncontainable lives. Our messes sometimes accompany us to work. Our flaws emerge, and our anxieties overflow. Our personalities, as well as the personalities of those around us, are not readily moulded.

Do I fit in at work? Is my career a good fit for me? What changes can I make? What changes can I reasonably expect those around me to make? How human are any of us permitted to be? What are the boundaries? Who do I have a connection with? How do I deal with it? These appeared to be some of the questions Tyne was thinking about that day.

I know from experience that our armour can frequently benefit us— some of it will always be necessary—but I also believe that it may be defeated in many cases. Or, at the very least, exhausting. Wearing too much of it, being too defensive, too prepared for fight, will slow you down, interfering with how you move, your fluidity, and your ability to grow on the job. When you hide behind a mask, you can become estranged even from yourself. When you strive to be tough and invincible, you may miss out on developing genuine professional relationships that will help you grow, advance, and employ your complete set of skills. If you assume the worst of those around you, they will be more likely to assume the worst of you. Each decision we make has an associated cost. The bottom line is that if we spend a lot of time worrying about how we fit in and whether we belong—if we have to contort, alter, hide, and guard ourselves at work all the time—we risk missing out on opportunities to be seen as our best and truest selves, as expressive, fertile, and full of ideas. This is the difficulty and drain of feeling othered. Many of us are left considering those regal borders, the difficult-to-distinguish difference between reach and overreach. We must think carefully about our resources and how we spend them. Is it safe for me to speak out in a meeting? Is it acceptable to give a point of view or potential solution to an issue that is shaped by my uniqueness? Will my ingenuity be viewed as disobedient? Will my point of view be viewed as disrespectful, an unwelcome challenge to the status quo?

When I first got to Washington in 2009, I had no idea how life in the White House functioned. But I did have some idea of what it's like to start a new job. I'd done it before, and I'd also overseen a lot of new employees in the various managerial roles I'd held. After working in law, city government, the charity sector, and healthcare, I knew that you don't just go into a new job and expect it to be perfect for you. You must conduct study, take a step back, and think strategically while you learn and adjust to your new work. To put it another way, you must toe the line before you can even consider attempting to redraw it.

I've previously discussed how being the First Lady of the United States is a peculiar and strangely powerful kind of non-job. It does not include a pay, a supervisor, or an employee handbook. I was motivated to get it right as a lifetime box checker. I planned to arrive prepared. After Barack was elected president, I immediately set about learning what was expected of me and how I could do the best job possible while also bringing my own enthusiasm and originality to the job. And I reasoned that if I did it well enough, I might be able to shift some of the perceptions about the role.

One of the first things I did was ask my new chief of staff to look through Laura Bush's official schedule, day by day and week by week, collecting a list of appearances she'd made and activities she'd planned. My strategy was to spend the first year doing everything Laura had done while also building my own set of priorities and plans for launching initiatives. Meanwhile, I will not be caught using any shortcuts. This was another instrument, a type of insurance policy. I was conscious of the tightrope I'd be walking as the first Black woman in the position. I was well aware that I would have to earn my way into acceptance. That meant I'd have to sharpen my perfection. I wanted to make sure everyone knew I was capable of carrying out every single responsibility I'd inherited, so I wouldn't be accused of being lazy or dismissive of the role.

Many of the First Lady's responsibilities, it turned out, had been accumulated over hundreds of years of custom. Nothing was written down; the expectations were simply built into the role. From state dinners to the annual Easter Egg Roll, I was meant to host a variety of activities. Every year, I was expected to have tea with the wives of visiting dignitaries and to provide vision for holiday décor. Otherwise, I could choose which causes I wanted to support and which concerns I wanted to address.

What I hadn't expected were some of the subtler, less-spoken-about expectations that seemed to come with the area. As we prepared for Barack's inauguration, I was informed, for example, that the four First Ladies directly preceding me had worn beautiful purses designed by the same New York designer on Inauguration Day. Oscar de la Renta, another legendary designer, liked to boast about how he'd clothed every First Lady since Betty Ford, which meant he'd assume the same about me. Nobody was forcing me to make any of these decisions, but the assumptions seemed to float around in the air.

As Barack and I settled into a historic home and these historic duties, there was a sense that things had always been done a certain way, that even some of the tiny customs existed as a type of honour, a gentle manner of continuity transmitted from one age to the next.

Any refusal to follow them looked to be tinged with arrogance. And if you grew up Black in America, you are well aware of the hazards of being perceived as arrogant.

I did not carry the required brand of purse on Inauguration Day, and I waited six years to wear anything by Oscar de la Renta, instead choosing to use my platform to highlight the brilliance of underrepresented designers. These were decisions I felt comfortable making, lines I was delighted to draw, partly because they concerned my own appearance, what I put on my own body. But I remained cautious about my image, my words, my ideas, and my projects. I was cautious in every decision I made, cognizant of the consequences of perceived overreach. To some, the fact that we'd made it to the White House at all felt radical, like a challenge to the existing order. We realised that if we wanted to move forward, we had to be careful with how we gained and spent our credibility.

Barack's bequest included two complex foreign conflicts and a looming economic slump that was becoming worse by the week. The West Wing communications team made it quite obvious that his success was, at least in part, dependent on me. (If you make a mistake, we all make a mistake.) Any gaffe from me—any flub, any statement or professional move that drew criticism—could potentially dent Barack's approval rating with the public, reducing his clout with legislators and derailing his efforts to get important bills passed in Congress, which could then translate to losing his reelection bid, which would cost many people in the administration their jobs. Furthermore, I was conscious that if the first non-white president failed or otherwise flamed out, it might potentially close and lock the door for future candidates of colour.

Those warnings rang in my thoughts as I wandered around. They were present whenever I spoke with a reporter or introduced a new project as First Lady. They were with me anytime I stood in front of an audience and saw the sea of lofted cellphone cameras, all those hundreds of small false mirrors held up, all those individual impressions formed.

But I realised that if I worried about such things too much, I'd never be able to be myself. I needed to draw a line between other people's concerns and my own. I had to trust my instincts, recall my own core, and avoid being too rigid with self-consciousness, anxious, or defensive. What I sought to do was maintain my agility by alternating between the known coasts of caution and recklessness. I lived by the code I learned growing up on Euclid Avenue, one that prioritised preparedness and adaptability over fear. But, all the while, I was dealing with another label, an even more pernicious one that I couldn't seem to shake.

CHAPTER 9

GOING HIGH

When Barack ran for president, I got a swift and painful education in how prejudices get reconstructed as "truth." The more I campaigned for him in public, and the more important I became, the more I saw my motions and words perverted, and my facial expressions converted into cartoons. My ardent belief in my husband's campaign, the notion that he had something to offer our country, was frequently portrayed as an unseemly form of rage.

If you believed some of the images and right-wing talk, I was a full-fledged, fire-breathing monster. I wandered around with my forehead wrinkled, continuously enraged. This, regrettably, corresponded to a bigger, more established attitude that academics have lately discovered in workplace studies: If a Black woman exhibits anything like anger, people are more inclined to dismiss it as a basic personality trait rather than as a result of any form of instigating scenario, making her simpler to marginalise and dismiss. Anything you do—any action you take—can be interpreted as crossing a line. In fact, you may be considered as merely living on the wrong side of the law. When that label is applied, all context is lost: Angry Black Woman! That's exactly who you are!

This is similar to how the term "ghetto" is applied to a neighbourhood. It's a quick and efficient dismissal, a coded bit of bias warning others to keep away, to recede in fear, and to invest elsewhere. It ignores your wealth, vibrancy, individuality, and potential, instead relegating you to the margins. What happens if being on the periphery irritates you? What if living in an uninvested-in community causes you to act like someone who is indeed boxed in and desperate? So, your action now merely supports and reinforces the stereotype, further boxing you in and delegitimizing anything you would say about any of it. You may find yourself without a voice and unheard, living out the failures that others have assigned for you.

It's a horrible sensation. And it's one I'm familiar with. No matter how calm I remained or how hard I worked as First Lady, the perception of me as aggressive and angry, and hence unworthy of respect, felt virtually impossible to overcome at times. When I began speaking publicly about our country's childhood obesity epidemic and advocating for relatively simple changes we could make to provide more healthy food options at school in 2010, a group of prominent conservative commentators seized on the old stereotype and used it to attack. They portrayed me as an overbearing, fist-waving destroyer set on destroying children's happiness and poking my nose where it didn't belong. They recommended that I throw people in jail for eating French fries. I was advocating for a government-mandated diet. From there, the conspiracies easily spread outward. "If the government is allowed to dictate our diet, what's next?" one Fox News commentator said. "Do they start deciding who we'll marry, where we'll work?" Of course, none of this was real. However, when lies are placed on top of well ingrained preconceptions, they become significantly simpler to sustain. Undoing stereotypes is arduous and time-consuming work. I rapidly noticed there were traps all throughout the place. If I tried to confront the stereotype directly, in a cheerful, happy interview (in this case, with Gayle King on CBS This Morning in 2012), here's what I got:

Could I be irritated by being perceived as perpetually irritated? I could, but who would benefit from it? How powerful could I possibly become then? Instead, I was forced to go high.

There is one question that I get asked more frequently and predictably than any other. Almost every time I chat to an interviewer or sit down with a new group of people, someone raises their hand, while others lean forward to listen.

What exactly does it mean to go high?

It appears that I could spend years answering this question. So let me give it a shot here.

I first said the words "When they go low, we go high" in public during a speech at the 2016 Democratic National Convention in Philadelphia. Hillary Clinton and Donald Trump were both running for president. My job was to mobilise Democratic voters, reminding them to stay involved and do the work necessary to elect their candidate, including voting on Election Day. As I frequently do, I discussed how the issues of the day were important to me as a father to my two daughters, and how the decisions Barack and I made were always guided by the ideas we wanted our children to perceive as vital.

To be honest, I had no clue that the expression "we go high" would become nearly synonymous with my name in the years to come. All I was really doing was giving a basic mantra that my family tries to live by, a handy bit of shorthand. When we observed people losing their integrity, Barack and I would remind ourselves to keep ours. "Going high" was a term used to indicate a decision we were making to try more and think more. It was a distillation of our ideas, a soup pot full of ingredients taken from our upbringings and simmered into us through time: Tell the truth, do your best for others, maintain perspective, and remain tough. That's basically our survival strategy.

Privately, Barack and I have committed and recommitted to the idea of going high numerous times, particularly as we have navigated life in the public glare through difficult campaigns and political struggles. We invoke it whenever we feel we are being tried, as a reminder to remain calm when faced with a moral problem. What do you do when everyone else is at their worst? How does one react when they are attacked? Sometimes it's quite easy to know, the answers are completely plain, and other times it's more difficult, the conditions are more ambiguous, and the proper path requires more contemplation.

Going high is like putting a line in the sand, a barrier we can create and then pause to examine. Which side do I want to be on in this? It's a summons to pause and reflect, to answer with both your heart and your head. Going high, in my opinion, is always a test. That is why I felt obligated to raise the concept in front of all those people at the 2016 convention: We were being tested as a nation. We were up against a moral quandary. We were being asked to answer. It wasn't the first time, and it certainly wouldn't be the last.

But, I suppose, the problem with any simple motto is that it is often easier to remember and repeat (or to emblazon on a coffee mug or T-shirt, tote bag, baseball cap, set of No. 2 pencils, stainless-steel water bottle, pair of athleisure leggings, pendant necklace, or wall tapestry, all of which can be found for sale on the internet) than to put into active daily practice.

Don't worry about the minor details? Maintain your cool and carry on?

Yes, yes, and yes to all of it. But please explain how. When people ask me to explain what it means to go high these days, I sometimes sense a slightly less polite question riding on its backside, tinged by natural scepticism, a feeling brewed by weariness and arriving when our efforts seem futile and our tests don't end: But wait, have you seen the world lately? Can things be much worse? Where is the will to fight?

People wrote to me when George Floyd died on a Minneapolis street corner with a police officer's knee on his neck in May 2020, questioning whether going high was truly the appropriate answer. They thought something similar after the Capitol building was attacked, when Republican officials continued to endorse false and destabilising accusations about our elections. The possibilities are limitless. More than a million Americans have died in a pandemic that exposes every flaw in our civilization. The Russian military has slaughtered civilians in Ukraine. In Afghanistan, the Taliban has prohibited girls from attending school. While communities are constantly ravaged by gun violence and hate crime in the United States, our own politicians have pushed to outlaw abortion. Transgender rights, LGBT rights, voting rights, and women's rights are still under attack. Every time there is another injustice, another round of brutality, another instance of failing leadership, corruption, or a violation of rights, I receive letters and emails asking the same question.

Is it still appropriate to get high?

So, how about now?

Yes, in my opinion. Yes, it is still true. We must continue to strive for greater heights. We must commit and recommit to the concept. Working with integrity is important. It will be remembered forever. It is merely a tool.

At the same time, I want to be clear: getting high is something you do, not something you feel. It is not a call to remain complacent and wait for change, or to stand by and watch others struggle. It is not about accepting oppressive conditions or allowing cruelty and power to go uncontested. Going high should not raise any questions about whether we are obligated to fight for more fairness, decency, and justice in the world; rather, it is about how we fight, how we approach solving problems, and how we sustain ourselves long enough to be effective rather than burn out. Some perceive this as an unfair and ineffective compromise, an extension of respectability politics in which we must submit to the rules rather than oppose them in order to survive. Why, people ask, do we have to strive to be so sensible all the time?

I can see how some people believe that reason excludes wrath. I get the impression that getting high means removing yourself from things that may otherwise irritate and provoke you. But it's not at all like that. I was neither distant nor unbothered when I spoke those words on the convention stage in Philadelphia in 2016. I was actually rather agitated. I had been fully inflamed by the bile spewing from the mouths of Republican officials on a regular basis at that point. I was tired of witnessing my husband's work and integrity belittled for nearly eight years, including prejudiced attempts to throw his citizenship into question. (I'll say it again: I don't think you're entitled to what you have.) And I was enraged that the main cause of that intolerance was now running for president.

But where was my true strength? I knew it wasn't in my hurt and wrath, at least not in their raw or unfiltered forms. My power resided in whatever I could do with that hurt and wrath, where I could take it, and where I could send it. It all came down to whether I could turn those rawer emotions into something that others would find difficult to dismiss, which was a clear message, a call to action, and a result I was prepared to fight towards.

Going high is what it is for me. It's about converting an abstract and frequently upsetting sentiment into some type of tangible plan, to get through the raw things and toward a greater answer.

I want to emphasise that this is a process that is not always swift. It may require some time and patience. It's normal to simmer for a while, to dwell inside the turmoil created by injustice, fear, or loss, or to vent your pain. It's fine to give yourself the time and space you need to recover or heal. Going high for me usually entails pausing before reacting. It is a type of self-control, a line drawn between our finest and worst instincts. Going high is about avoiding the desire to engage in shallow wrath and corrosive contempt and instead figuring out how to reply to whatever is shallow and toxic around you with a clear voice. It's what happens when you turn a reaction into a response.

Because consider this: Emotions are not strategies. They don't solve problems or make amends. You can feel them—you will, inevitably—but be cautious about allowing them to guide you. Rage can be compared to a filthy windshield. Hurt is analogous to a broken steering wheel. Disappointment will merely sit in the back seat, sullen and unhelpful. They'll lead you straight into a ditch if you don't do something positive with them.

My power has always been dependent on my ability to keep myself out of trouble.

When people ask me about climbing high, I tell them that it's about doing whatever it takes to make your job count and your voice heard, despite the odds. It helps if you can remain flexible and adjust to change as it occurs. And all of that, I've discovered, becomes more achievable when you're prepared and practised with a comprehensive set of tools. Going high is not only about what happens on a single day, month, or election cycle. It occurs over the span of a lifetime, even a generation. Going high is a commitment to showing your children, friends, colleagues, and community what it is to live with love and function with decency. Because, in the end, what you put out for others, whether it's hope or hatred, will only create more of the same.

But make no mistake: going high is work—often difficult, tiresome, uncomfortable, and bruising. You must ignore the naysayers and the sceptics. You'll need to put up some barriers between yourself and people who want you to fail. And you'll have to keep working when everyone else has become jaded or cynical and given up. John Lewis, the late civil rights leader, attempted to remind us of this. "Freedom is not a state; it is an act," he wrote once. "It's not some enchanted garden perched high on a distant plateau where we can finally sit down and rest."

We live in an era when reacting has become almost too simple, almost too convenient. Hurt, disappointment, and terror spread quickly, as does rage. Both information and misinformation appear to be flowing at the same rate. Our thumbs get us in trouble by becoming convenient targets for our rage. We can type a few angry words and hurl them like rockets into the digital stratosphere, never knowing where, how, or who they will impact. And, yes, our wrath, like our grief, is frequently justified. The question is, what are we going to do with it? Can we tie it to discipline in order to produce something more permanent than noise? Complacency nowadays frequently wears the mask of convenience: we might click "like" or "repost" and then admire ourselves for being involved, or consider ourselves activists, after three seconds of effort. We've gotten good at making noise and applauding one another, but we occasionally forget to do the job. You may make an impact with a three-second investment, but you are not producing change.

Are we responding or reacting? It's worth considering from time to time. It's a question I ask myself before posting anything on social media or making any kind of public statement. Am I acting rashly, merely to make myself feel better? Have I connected my emotions to anything concrete and actionable, or am I simply being driven by them? Am I willing to put in the effort required to effect change?

When it comes to getting high, I find that the process of writing may be an extremely useful tool. It's a way for me to work through my emotions, sifting them into useful shape. Throughout Barack's campaign and my time in the White House, I was fortunate to work with talented speechwriters who would sit down with me and let me verbally dump my brain into theirs, taking notes as I worked through my most visceral feelings, assisting me in making sense of my thoughts and beginning to shape them.

Saying things aloud to a trusted listener has always encouraged me to put my ideas to the test in broad daylight. It enables me to untangle my rage and concerns and begin to seek a bigger explanation. I'm able to separate what's constructive from what isn't, resulting in a greater set of facts for myself. My earliest views, I've realised, are rarely all that valuable; they're simply the beginning point from which we move forward. After seeing everything on the paper, I continue to tweak, revise, and ponder, until arriving at something with a meaningful purpose. My writing process has evolved into one of the most effective instruments in my life.

If my first convention address in Denver in 2008 felt like a start, an on-ramp to my life as First Lady, the one I gave in 2016 felt more like a stop, the beginning of the end.

I had my message, my words, and my basic set of emotions. Everything was learned and well-practised in my thoughts. But, once again, something went wrong. It wasn't a malfunctioning teleprompter this time, but rather a spectacular summer rainstorm that decided to land over Philadelphia just as my jet was about to take off.

I was travelling with a small group of staffers and was about to begin my convention speech in about an hour when the air became rough, judging us in our seats. The voice of our Air Force pilot came over the microphone, urging everyone to belt up. He mentioned that we would have to reroute our landing to Delaware owing to the weather. This instantly sparked fear among members of my team about how to deal with the delay: I was the main speaker at the convention that night, the anchor around whom the prime-time schedule had been crafted.

The juddering was only an appetiser, since the jet heaved strongly to one side a minute or so later, as if it were being flicked out of the way by some giant night-monster floating somewhere out there in the pouring rain. For a few seconds, it appeared as if we were falling, sideways and down, completely out of control. As lightning blazed outside our windows and the plane jackhammered into the clouds, I heard people around me begin to scream and sob. I could see the faint lights of a city below. I wasn't planning on dying. I simply wanted to deliver that speech.

I was about eight years into my tenure as First Lady at this point. I'd sat by the bedsides of military service personnel who were attempting to recover from horrific war injuries. I'd grieved with a mother whose fifteen-year-old daughter had been fatally murdered on her way home from school in a Chicago park. I'd stood inside Nelson Mandela's tiny jail cell, where he'd spent the better part of twenty-seven years alone and still found the strength to carry on. We'd celebrated the Affordable Care Act's enactment, the Supreme Court's support of marriage equality, and hundreds of other minor and significant victories. And I'd gone to the Oval Office and wrapped my arms around Barack, both of us speechless and crushed, on the day a gunman murdered twenty elementary school pupils dead in Connecticut.

The reality we lived in has repeatedly perplexed, humbled, and shook me, bringing me down and then raising me back up. I'd been exposed to what seemed like every aspect of the human condition, pummelling by alternating waves of joy and anguish, constantly reminded that little was predictable and that for every couple of steps forward, something would inevitably tear open old wounds and set us all back.

I couldn't go a day without thinking of my father and the disease that had gradually robbed him of his strength and mobility, the patience and grace he'd shown when dealing with the emotional and physical challenges it brought—the way he'd continued to show up for his family, renewing his sense of hope and possibility on a daily basis in order to move forward. He'd mapped out what "going high" looked like for me. I realised what we were up against as a country in 2016, the struggle of another election and a decision that felt more stark than anything I'd known. I felt agitated while on that plane. I was concerned. I was also armoured. If anything was going to throw me off course at this point, it had to be far bigger than a layer of unstable air over Philadelphia. We made it to the ground safely. We arrived at the convention centre. I quickly changed into my dress, heels, and lipstick and walked onto that stage. I gathered my courage, double-checked the teleprompters and the confidence monitor, smiled and waved to the audience, and then began to talk.

It may seem unusual to imply that after doing it once or twice, you might begin to feel comfortable playing in front of a stadium-sized crowd, but it is real. Or, perhaps more precisely, you become acclimated to the discomfort of performance. You become accustomed to being terrified. The nerve-racking zing of adrenaline, all the uncertainties that come with performing in front of a live and worked-up audience, they start to have less of an impact on you than they used to. The whole experience comes to resemble fuel rather than terror. Especially when you have something important to convey.

My address that night in Philadelphia was as moving as the one I'd given in Denver all those years before. What was different was that we were about to go. Whatever happened at that convention or in the election that followed, regardless of who became president, my family would be leaving the White House in approximately six months and going on vacation. We'd be dusting our hands off the whole presidential attempt one way or another.

That evening, I was overcome with emotion. But I was trying to organise them all into a strategy. I reminded everyone that no decision had been made. We couldn't afford to be exhausted, upset, or pessimistic about the upcoming election, I remarked. We had no choice except to go for broke. And we'd have to earn the victory by knocking on doors and registering voters. I concluded my remarks by stating, "So let's get to work."

Then I returned to the airport and boarded the jet, taking off into the still-uncertain air.

What I said that evening may have contributed to the expression "When they go low, we go high" becoming part of the zeitgeist, but the rest didn't transfer. Too many of us who heard the call forgot to perform the task. On Election Day 2016, more than 90 million eligible voters did not vote. And with that, we drove ourselves into a ditch. We had to live with the results for four years. We are still living with them.

How do we get our bearings in the midst of a raging storm? How do we find stability when the air around us is turbulent and the earth beneath our feet appears to shift constantly? I believe it starts, in part, when we can discover a feeling of agency and purpose in the midst of constant fluctuation, when we realise that modest power may be meaningful power. Voting is important. It is important to assist a neighbour. Giving your time and energy to a cause you believe in is important. It is important to speak up when you notice an individual or group of people being denigrated or dehumanised. It is important to express your joy for another human, whether it is your child, a coworker, or simply someone you pass on the street. Your modest activities become a tool for increasing your visibility, solidity, and sense of connection. They can help you remember that you, too, are important.

The challenges that surround us are only increasing. We will need to reestablish our confidence in other people in order to reclaim some of our lost faith—all of which has been shaken out of us in recent years. Nothing is accomplished on its own. Little of it will happen if we isolate ourselves within our pockets of sameness, communicating solely with those who share our same viewpoints and talking more than listening.

The online magazine Slate produced a story with the headline "Is 2016 the Worst Year in History?," noting everything from Trump's apparent popularity to police killings, the Zika virus, and Brexit as potential evidence. But, you see, we hadn't yet met 2017, which became, according to press coverage of a Gallup global study on emotional health, "The World's Worst Year in at Least a Decade."

This was followed, of course, by a new year and then another, each one marked by new crises and disasters. Time magazine dubbed 2020 "The Worst Year Ever," though many would argue that 2021 was no better. The idea is that uncertainty is a constant; we will continue to strive, to face anxiety, and to seek some sense of control. We won't always be able to find our bearings inside the historical moment we're in. Is the situation improving or deteriorating? Who is it for? And how do we even quantify? What is a nice day for you may be a bad day for your neighbour. One country may thrive while another suffers. Joy and suffering frequently coexist; they intermingle. Most of us reside in the in-between, pursuing that most fundamental of human instincts, to cling to hope. We encourage one another not to give up. Continue your efforts. This is also important.

When I became a parent and started asking my own mother questions about how to parent well, one of the things she told me was, "Don't ever pretend that you have all the answers. It's okay to say 'I don't know.' "

I began this book by describing some of the questions I get asked by others. I will end it by reminding you that I don't actually have all that many answers to give. I believe that real answers come from longer, deeper dialogues—a conversation we all try to have together.

We can't know for sure what the future holds, but I do think it's important to remember that we are also not helpless in the face of our worries. We are capable of creating change by design, change that's a response to flux rather than a reaction to it. We can operate from hope rather than fear, pairing reason with rage. But we'll need to renew our sense of possibility many times over. I think of my father's silent credo any time his cane failed him and he crashed to the floor: You fall, you get up, you carry on.

A motto like "We go high" does nothing if we only just hear it and repeat it. We can't coast on words alone. We can't declare ourselves sad or angry or committed or hopeful and then just sit down and rest.

It's the kind of lesson we'll only continue to learn. As we saw in the 2016 election, it can be presumptuous to assume everything will work out in your favour, and dangerous to leave your fate entirely in the hands of others when it comes to choosing your leaders. We have to make hopeful choices, to commit and recommit to the work involved. Freedom is no enchanted garden, as John Lewis said. It's a barbell we keep hoisting overhead.

Sometimes going high might mean that you have to make a choice to operate inside of certain margins, even if the margins themselves are a provocation. You may need to climb partway up a grand staircase so that you can be better seen and heard when addressing the ballroom crowd.

While we were in the White House, I knew I had to stay armoured and also accept some of the trade-offs, understanding that I represented more than just myself. I needed to stick with my work, my plans, my hopes—to focus on action rather than reaction. Getting defensive would only backfire. I had to go about building my legitimacy and credibility somewhat slowly, detouring as best I could around the traps, keeping myself out of the ditch. Did this involve strategy and compromise? Yes, it did. Sometimes you have to clear the path in order to be able to walk on it yourself, as well as to ready it for others. As I've said, it's often tedious, inconvenient, and bruising work. But in my experience, this is what it takes if you're trying to enter a new frontier.

There's a type of question I get often from young people who are feeling both motivated and impatient, fed up with the way things are. It's a question that gets at the nature of activism, resistance, and change more generally: How much do we abide by and how much do we reject? Do we tear down our systems or try to stay patient and reform them from the inside? Are we more effective agitating for change at the margins or inside the mainstream? What does true boldness look like? When does civility become an excuse for inaction?

These are not new questions. It's not a new debate. Each generation rediscovers it on its own. And the answers aren't straightforward. Which is why the debate stays fresh, the questions remain open, and, if you're lucky, why your own kids and grandkids will come to you someday, burning with passion, frustrated and impatient and ready to challenge, pondering the very margins you tried to widen for them, asking these same questions all over again.

I was barely a year old when John Lewis and about six hundred other civil rights advocates marched across the Edmund Pettus Bridge in Selma, Alabama, enduring violent attacks by segregationist sheriff's deputies and state troopers while trying to draw attention to the need for voting rights to be protected by federal law. I was too young to remember the day Dr. Martin Luther King Jr. stood on the steps of the state capitol in Montgomery, addressing not just the 25,000 or so people who'd ultimately joined Lewis and the others on the march, but also a country that was finally paying attention to the struggle. What Dr. King said that day, among other things, was that the struggle was far from over, the destination far from reached. "I know you are asking today," he said to the crowd, " 'How long will it take?' "

While urging Americans to commit to nonviolence and continue striving for justice, and exhorting everyone to practise both faith and vigour, he responded, "Not for long." When we discuss the nature of change and progress, I sometimes think we're mostly debating the meaning of the phrase "Not for long." Is it a matter of years, decades, or generations to arrive at a state of fairness and peace? Do we take steps, strides, or leaps to get there? What strategies are necessary? What concessions are required? What sacrifices are made? What is the length of Not long?

When Barack's parents married in Hawaii in 1961, interracial marriage was outlawed in about half of the country, and it was prohibited in twenty-two states. It wasn't until I was 10 years old that American women were granted the legal ability to apply for a credit card without the agreement of their husbands. My grandpa grew up in the South during a time when Black people were shot simply for showing up to vote. I reflected about this whenever I stood on the Truman Balcony of the White House, watching my two dark-skinned daughters play on the grass.

As the first Black First Lady, I was a "only." It meant that I had to assist the world adapt and adjust to me while myself adapting and adjusting to the role. As president, Barack was doing much the same. We were unique, but not in a bad way. We had to demonstrate this to people over and over again, despite the threats to our integrity. We had to stay agile and stay out of the traps. Many people I know are challenged to educate, explain, and represent themselves at the same time in their personal and professional lives, even if they don't want or enjoy the extra labour. Patience, dexterity, and sometimes some extra armour are required.

Even though the White House seemed and felt like a mansion, I was still myself inside. I became more at ease in that environment, revealing more of myself with time. I could dance if I wanted to. I could also crack jokes if I wanted to. As I got to know the position better, I began to push the boundaries more, giving myself more leeway to be expressive and creative, and tying my work as First Lady more fully to my personality. This meant that I appeared on TV and had a good time dancing with Jimmy Fallon or doing push-ups with Ellen DeGeneres to promote Let's Move!, my children's health campaign. On the White House lawn, I could jump rope and play soccer with the youngsters. I could rap with a Saturday Night Live cast member to educate young people of the importance of pursuing a college education. My goal has always been to undertake serious work in a fun way, to show people what is possible if we continue to aim high.

I reasoned that the only way to combat an ugly stereotype was to be myself, to continually demonstrate how wrong it was, even if it took years and even if some people would never do anything but buy into it. At the same time, I attempted to stay committed to changing the mechanisms that had given rise to the stereotype in the first place. I had to wield my influence wisely and utilise my voice with care, hoping that it would only widen the margins for whoever came after. I knew I'd have a higher chance of success if I focused my attention only on fulfilling the goals I'd set for myself as First Lady, and if I avoided being distracted or distracted by those who would rather see me fail. It struck me as a challenge, a sort of moral test. As usual, I was carefully budgeting my energy and counted the steps.

Supreme Court Justice Ketanji Brown Jackson delivers a moving anecdote about her time as a Harvard undergraduate. She had arrived at school from south Florida in 1988, ready to study government. She enjoyed theatre and was eager to audition for roles. She also joined the Black Students Association.

The BSA swiftly planned a series of protests after a white student hung a Confederate flag in a dorm room window that faced one of the school quads. Jackson was part of a group of primarily Black students that dropped everything and began circulating petitions, handing out fliers, and assisting in the planning of rallies, which successfully placed pressure on the college administration and resulted in widespread media coverage across the United States. Their opposition was powerful, but the future Supreme Court justice was well aware of a potential trap.

"While we were busy doing all of those very noble things, we were not in the library studying," she subsequently explained. The cost of completing that work, of being put on the defence, was significant. It sapped their vitality and hindered them from attending play rehearsals, study halls, and social gatherings. It stopped them from being recognized as innovative, fertile, and full of new ideas in other fields. "I remember thinking at the time how unfair it was to us," she remarked.

It occurred to her at the time that this was part of bigotry's bigger mechanism, a technique of keeping outsiders from getting too far inside, to get them off the staircase and ejected out of the ballroom. It was "exactly what the student who hung the flag really wanted: for us to be so distracted that we failed our classes, reinforcing the stereotype that we couldn't cut it at a place like Harvard," she explained.

It's difficult to be on the outside looking in. Fighting for equity and justice from the outside is even more difficult. As a result, I believe you should pick your battles wisely, be mindful of your emotions, and consider your long-term goals. The most effective among us understand that this is significant in and of itself—a necessary aspect of getting high.

I frequently speak with young people who are debating how to best invest their energy, time, and resources. They are frequently under pressure, caught between worlds, suffering from survivor's guilt, having abandoned a family or a community to seek new aspirations. When you start to get someplace, individuals who have never seen you as different may begin to see you as different or altered. They believe that because you passed past the gates, you must now dwell in the palace. This adds another layer of complication. It gives you more options for navigating. More to discuss. You may receive a college scholarship and soon become the pride of your family or community, but that doesn't imply you can instantly pay your uncle's electric bill or return home every weekend to care for your grandmother or younger siblings. Success entails making many difficult decisions and drawing the lines that go with them, trusting that your efforts will pay off in the long run if you can stay on track. All you have to do is keep repeating yourself, "Not long."

According to Justice Jackson, the greatest thing her parents provided her as a child was toughness, a headstrong type of confidence. She learned to erect a mental wall between herself from the judgments of others, remaining steadfastly focused on her broader goals, refusing to be knocked off course by unfairness or hostility. She was raised with a distinctive African name, was often an "only" at school, and eventually worked in law. She attributes her accomplishment to three factors: hard effort, major breaks, and a thick skin. The thick-skin aspect entails understanding what to do with your wrath and hurt, where to channel it, and how to transform it into genuine power. It entails deciding on a destination and accepting that getting there will take some time. "The best thing you can do for yourself and your community is to stay focused," Jackson said a Black student group in 2020.

Going high is all about figuring out how to keep the poison out and the power in. It implies that you must use your energy wisely and be firm in your convictions. You press forward in some situations while pulling back in others, allowing yourself time to relax and recharge. It helps to remember that you, like everyone else, are on a budget. We work with a limited but renewable set of resources when it comes to our attention, our time, our reputation, and our goodwill toward and from others. Throughout our lives, we repeatedly fill and empty our pockets. We work, save, and spend our money.

When we were kids, my brother asked my father, "Are we rich?"

My father simply laughed and stated, "No." But the following time he earned a paycheck, instead of depositing it, he cashed it in, returning home with a large stack of dollars, which he then lay out on the foot of his bed so Craig and I could see every penny. There seemed to be a lot of them to me.

For a little moment, we appeared to be wealthy.

My father then went to find the stack of bills that arrived each month, and one by one, he opened the envelopes and explained how much we owed for what—this much for electricity, that much for the car payment, more for the gas that cooked our food and the groceries that filled our fridge. He began slipping the approximate amount of money due into the various envelopes, talking about the other things we paid for—gas in the car, rent to Aunt Robbie each month, new clothes for school, our annual summertime week at a family resort in Michigan, and some savings for the future.

He brought down the pile of cash, bill by bill, until there was only a solitary twenty lying on the bed, meant to represent the money we had left over for luxuries like ice cream and drive-in movies.

My father told us that we weren't wealthy, but we were wise. We were cautious. We were quite aware. We could see the edge, but we weren't going to cross it. He was attempting to demonstrate to us that if we were prudent with our expenditures, we would always be fine. We were going to get ice cream. We'd watch movies. We'd get to college eventually. Our foresight enabled us to arrive.

This strategy guided my work as First Lady, as I remained cognizant of my resources—how much I had to offer and how much I still had to earn. I tried to be strategic in my efforts, sticking to actionable ideas and leaving the irrational rage to others. I put on the most protective armour I could find. I maintained my physical fitness. I ate well and made sleep a priority. I nourished my pleasure and sense of stability by spending time with friends and family, relying on the power of my Kitchen Table. When my terrified mind began to race, I spoke back to it, quieting it down. When I felt my emotions boiling over—when anything made me angry, upset, and ready to explode—I took some time to process those thoughts privately, often utilising my mother and friends as sounding boards, trying to come up with better solutions.

I was well aware of my situation. I recognized myself. I also realised that I couldn't be everything to everyone. This helped me to remain calm in the face of harsh comments and misinterpretations. I was aware of my priorities and had years of experience setting boundaries, which enabled me to say "no" plainly but gracefully to many of the requests that came in. I embraced the power of tiny by narrowing my focus, deciding to work on a few core topics that were important to me while remaining committed to my family. And I tried to be gentle with myself, to guard and share my light while drawing on the limitless light supplied by others, the many individuals I met along the journey, all throughout this beautiful and shattered globe.

When I sensed my stress level rising or my cynicism rising, I made it a point to visit a school or invite a group of children to the White House, which quickly restored any lost perspective and helped explain my purpose all over again. For me, children are a constant reminder that we are all born kind and open-minded, devoid of hatred. They are the reason the rest of us keep our cool and keep attempting to clear the route. When you see a child develop into an adult, you realise how commonplace and deep the process can be, how it may happen slowly and quickly all at once, in stages and strides. You begin to understand what Not long means.

My girls like looking through old family photos and laughing at what they see—not just pictures of themselves as charming babies or enjoying little-kid birthday parties, but also older ones. They could chuckle if they saw a picture of me when I was seventeen, with an Afro and clad head to toe in 1980s denim, or a picture of Barack as a round-faced youngster plunging in shallow seas in Hawaii. Or they'll marvel at a sepia-toned image of my mother, appearing youthful and stylish in the late 1950s. They'll say we appear just like ourselves, finding the stability through time to be nearly miraculous.

The contents of this book may not be copied, reproduced or transmitted without the express written permission of the author or publisher. Under no circumstances will the publisher or author be responsible or liable for any damages, compensation or monetary loss arising from the information contained in this book, whether directly or indirectly. .

Disclaimer Notice:

Although the author and publisher have made every effort to ensure the accuracy and completeness of the content, they do not, however, make any representations or warranties as to the accuracy, completeness, or reliability of the content. , suitability or availability of the information, products, services or related graphics contained in the book for any purpose. Readers are solely responsible for their use of the information contained in this book

Every effort has been made to make this book possible. If any omission or error has occurred unintentionally, the author and publisher will be happy to acknowledge it in upcoming versions.

Printed in Great Britain
by Amazon

35974789R00073